Advice to a Son

by NATHANIEL BLADEN

Editor: Karen Proudler

First Published in Great Britain in 2015
by Karen & Graham Proudler
Forge Cottage, Field Farm, Aston Lane, Shardlow
Derbys DE72 2GX
Copyright © 2015 Karen Proudler
All rights reserved.
ISBN: 978-0-9566831-8-2

All dates prior to 1752 are old style unless stated otherwise

ACKNOWLEDGEMENTS

With thanks to the Folger Shakespeare Library,
in Washington, D.C., USA for permission to transcribe
'Advice to a Son' from the original document they hold

CONTENTS

INTRODUCTION

'Advice to a Son'[1] was written in 1694 by a 52 year old Yorkshireman called Nathaniel Bladen for his youngest son, Martin, who was 14 years of age and about to go off to Westminster School. The father had no idea which direction his son's life would take him, but clearly felt the time was right to commit his advice to writing and, in case of his death, his son would thereby always have a written record of his father's guiding advice on the various challenges he might face in his life.

There is no doubt that Bladen's book was inspired by the then popular 'Advice to a Son. Or, Directions for Your Better Conduct Through the Various and Most Important Encounters of this Life' by Francis Osborne, the first part of which was published in 1656. Though well received and popular, reaction to Osborne's book, in some quarters where it was believed to have encouraged atheism, led to it being suppressed which, of course, led to it becoming even more popular and the second part of the book was published in 1658.

Bladen's 'Advice' has never been published

---

[1] Original manuscript held by the Folger Shakespeare Library in Washington DC, USA. Reference V.a. 346

before,[1] which is a shame because it gives a fascinating insight into the wisdom, values and principles of a late 17th century lawyer, who divided his time between the Inns of Court in London and his country residence in Hemsworth, Yorkshire. Born in the year Civil War broke out, Nathaniel's half century of living, which led up to the manuscript's production, were eventful, sometimes tragic and it was a life rich with experiences and setbacks, some of which, no doubt, he wished to spare his son the pain of discovering.

Bladen's 'Advice' is a book of two halves: the first being the advice and words of wisdom he composed himself amounting to some 11,000 words. The second part contains a translation of Lucian's De Mercede Conductis "Of the Inconveniences they suffer that serve in Noble Familys", the inclusion of which seems to demonstrate the author's greatest fear that his son should follow in his footsteps and enter into the service of a noble family. This was a subject close to Nathaniel's heart and its inclusion is seen as a warning to his son of the realities of such a life and that it should be avoided.

As will be explained in this Introduction, Nathaniel had suffered as a servant to several noble families and was emphatically trying to steer his son

---

[1] Two books, published by the Editor in July 2015 include citations from it: 'Martin Bladen: A Biography' and its companion book 'Early Yorkshire Bladens', both by Karen Proudler

away from the same path. With elegant understatement, indeed with no statement, the mere inclusion of Lucian's translation spoke volumes to his son, who would have been well aware of its significance.

Nathaniel's reasons for wanting to commit his 'Advice' to writing can be easily understood by a brief examination of his own childhood. His father and grandparents had resided for some time at Denton/Askwith at, or near, Denton Hall, the home of Lord Fairfax to whom Nathaniel's father had been a servant/steward in the 1630s. His father, who had been so closely involved with handling the affairs of the Fairfax family was later accused by Thomas, 3rd Lord Fairfax, of being a turncoat in the Civil War and he faced delinquency charges. Nathaniel's mother died at his birth, or shortly after and his father was dead by the time he was 3 years of age.

After his parents' deaths, Nathaniel's care was shared among relatives until he was old enough to go off to school. After the death of his grandmother, an aunt stepped in to care for him and she immediately brought legal action, on the boy's behalf, over the estate he inherited from his Birkhead grandfather[1]. In later years, in Nathaniel's correspondence to a close friend, he was to lament that he was left with no writings from his family to

---

[1] Bladen v Watson, 1655 TNA: C22/768/14

guide him and this seems to be what motivated him to ensure, should anything happen to him, that his young son Martin would have the benefit of his 'Advice'.

Nathaniel asked a family friend, Robert Wrightson, to assist him manage the estates he had inherited from his relations whilst he completed his education and became a lawyer. Wrightson was seen by some, certainly by Nathaniel's mother-in-law, as a sharp lawyer who took advantage of Nathaniel's youth and trust to acquire his property. To Nathaniel, however, he was a true friend and father-figure who remained his friend for life.

In due course Nathaniel married, making a highly advantageous marriage to Isabella Fairfax, a cousin of Lord Fairfax. Perhaps due to the influence of his new in-laws, he shortly afterwards became Steward to Thomas Osborne (later Earl of Danby, Marquess of Carmarthen and Duke of Leeds) and his family. Danby was a rising star and, during Bladen's long employment, he rose to become the most powerful politician of the day.

Bladen watched as Danby's climb to dizzying heights in government came under attack from his enemies who took the first opportunity to undermine him and there were calls for Danby's impeachment. Throughout the Popish Plot and Danby's imprisonment, Bladen was there doing his bidding, working with those involved as Danby's eyes and ears.[1]

Nathaniel experienced, first hand, what it was like to be in the service of one of the most illustrious men of the day, though Danby was despised by many of his contemporaries. This makes the emphasis placed by Bladen on the Lucian translation showing the dreadful pitfalls of serving a noble family so intriguing.

To understand why the Lucian translation is included with Nathaniel's 'Advice to a Son', but without a single reference to it being made by him, it is necessary to understand Bladen's situation in 1694. As Steward to Danby and the Osborne family and, despite his enormous difficulties with them, he was still engaged in service to them at the time, therefore it would have been hazardous for him to commit to writing any overt criticism of Danby who was now the King's principal adviser. Others were less reticent in expressing their opinion on Danby. John Evelyn, a life-long acquaintance, described him as 'a man of excellent natural parts but nothing of generous or grateful'; another contemporary, the Earl of Shaftesbury, called him "an inveterate liar, who was proud, ambitious, revengeful, false, prodigal and covetous to the

---

[1] Letters between Nathaniel Bladen and Thomas Knox and Lord Danby, ©The British Library Board, Add. MS 28049 ff24, 26, 40, 109 and 196. Also: The Tryal and Conviction of Thomas Knox and John Lane for a Conspiracy to Defame and Scandalize Dr Oates and Mr Bedloe thereby to discredit their evidence about the horrid Popish Plot; at the King's Bench Bar at Westminster, on Tuesday 25th November 1679

highest degree". He was said to be arrogant and that his wife was a domineering tyrant.[1]

The reference to Danby having a 'tyrannical wife' may explain the inclusion in Nathaniel's work of a poem "To the Countess of Danby upon the happy recovery of the Earl Danby from his late sickness".[2] If the Countess was as domineering of her husband as contemporary reports indicate, then Nathaniel may have found flattering her sensibilities a way to keep Danby's support.

Indeed, Nathaniel was careful not to write anything derogatory whatsoever about that family he was so closely allied to, at least nothing written by his own hand. By 1694 Danby was once again ascending to high political office and restored to power in King William's Court. He had also been made Duke of Leeds in May of that year, in addition to his other titles.

It would, at that time, have been the height of folly for Bladen to have put in writing the slightest criticism of Danby. Yet, if one is able to read between the lines and weigh up the significance of Lucian's translation featuring so prominently with the 'Advice', then it is clear that Nathaniel went as far as he felt able to by graphically demonstrating

---

[1] 'Early Yorkshire Bladens' by Karen Proudler, 2015
[2] Thomas Osborne 1632-1712 married in 1651 to Bridget Bertie c1629-1704, daughter of Montagu Bertie, 2nd Earl of Lindsey. Danby was frequently ill during his life, particularly in during the summer of 1673 when it was reported he was recovering from serious illness and again in 1684 - both times Bladen was in his service

the wretchedness of noble service, without in any way pointing the finger at a particular individual. Son Martin would not have failed to realise the significance, yet Nathaniel preserved his personal safety by not committing his own thoughts to paper yet made his feelings explicit by using a third party's experience which, in the style of a work heavily predicated on metaphor, seems appropriate.

Not long before he wrote his 'Advice', Nathaniel had suffered at the hands of Danby's children. Whilst working, again in his capacity as Steward, for Danby's daughter the Countess of Plymouth, she had accused Nathaniel of embezzlement. She had put an advertisement in The Gazette advertising his theft and brought about his imprisonment in Southwark debtors jail awaiting trial. All this occurred after she had locked him up in her house in Duke Street, London, for a period of days. During this incarceration her brother (Danby's son Latimer) and other men (servants) had threatened to cut Nathaniel's throat if he did not confess to the theft. [1] These difficulties with the Osborne family ran on for some considerable time but Bladen became engulfed in other difficulties too. He had his fingers burned over business dealings with Lady Theodosia Ivy, the infamous forger, who duped him and left him out of pocket.

---

[1] TNA: C9/11/117/25 Plymouth, Countess Dowager v Bladen, 1686

His dealings with other members of the nobility likewise seemed to have difficulties: he claimed the Duke of Buckingham (whose wife was a close cousin of Nathaniel's wife Isabella Fairfax) had promised him and his family life annuities but had inconveniently died before it was properly set in place. The Duke left his estate in such a poor state that his widow was unable to continue the Bladen annuity and it was stopped. Nathaniel's daughters claimed[1] they were facing financial ruin as a result. Even his own mother-in-law, Lady Fairfax, brought a Chancery Complaint against him regarding the advowson of Hemsworth Church.

All of which makes one wonder just how well qualified Nathaniel Bladen was to be dispensing advice. Yet, it was perhaps all those obstacles and set-backs that meant Bladen was particularly well suited to give advice, if, as seems likely, he learned from his adversity and emerged from his difficulties with fighting spirit and fortitude. It would then be natural for him to wish his young son to be spared from exposure to the same rigors.

Perhaps not surprisingly, a degree of cynicism permeates his 'Advice' on certain subjects and some of his comments seem harsh; such as, 'look on friends as future enemies.' These comments betray Nathaniel's own wariness where, from being a child trusting in all, he had learned the hard way to be

---

[1] TNA: C5/310/9 Bladen v Ash, 1700

careful in choosing friends. Either that, or he had been reading the same book as his son Martin, who will be discussed shortly. Martin had been absorbing Niccolò Machiavelli's 'The Prince' and was so impressed by certain passages that he added them to the manuscript.

When he wrote his Advice in 1694, Nathaniel had suffered the loss of his wife who died of typhoid fever in 1691, followed soon after by his mother-in-law Lady Fairfax and, in 1692, his eldest son William had moved to Maryland to take up an appointment on the Colonial Council. His eldest daughters were married and the youngest were about to be, so the family home in Yorkshire, which had once housed eight family members, was emptying rapidly.

Despite his close connection with the Osborne family, it seems doubtful Nathaniel knew Francis Osborne (the author of the original 'Advice') as Bladen did not marry into the Fairfax family or become engaged by Danby until after Francis Osborne's death, but he may have known John Osborne (the son and recipient of the 'Advice'). John Osborne was trained in the law, being called to the bar in 1657 and, as a successful barrister, may well have known Bladen who was attending the Inner Temple at this time.

The popularity of Osborne's 'Advice' continued after his death, from the 1660s through to the early

1720s and Nathaniel had obviously read it, digested Osborne's material and had been motivated to produce his own version for his young son.

Bladen followed the same structure of addressing topics: studies, love/marriage, religion etc. in an orderly fashion but then adopted the style of the Elizabethan, Francis Bacon to deliver the words with the most formal tone he could muster. The way Nathaniel expressed himself in this 'Advice' is different to any other writings he left. It was truly personal material that he was considering; yes, the topic was prompted by Osborne, but the style of expression was influenced by the Renaissance and the fluidic prose, full of learned words of wisdom, was pure Bacon. Short, terse sentences full of profound statements which were intended to make the reader think, and absorb the wisdom, to learn Bladen's lessons. It was rhetorical language which delivered maxim-like pronouncements but Bladen kept the recipient in mind throughout and referenced his metaphors and analogies to the boy's current studies and Ancient Greek mythology.

Imitation being the sincerest form of flattery, there is a degree of paraphrasing in Bladen's work that showed his approval of some of Osborne's points. Such as when Osborne[1] stated "Let not an

---

[1] Advice to a Son by Francis Osborne with an Introduction and Notes by His Honour Judge Edward Abbott Parry, 1896

over-passionate prosecution of Learning draw you from making an honest Improvement of your Estate". To which Bladen echoed "And all ye philosophy in Aristotle & Plato, or ye Sublime theorems of the Scholar will not pay one debt."

Osborne's earlier Advice caused much offence in his comments on woman-kind, with some labelling him a woman-hater and misogynistic. Bladen does not, however, emulate Osborne's intemperate language or sentiments but does reiterate the importance of making a good match with a woman with a portion and endorsed Osborne's advice to avoid a 'Celebrated Beauty'. He qualified this, however, with an earnest desire for his son to marry for affection but cautioned that, in time, the passion would cool.

Although Nathaniel was the principal author of 'Advice to a Son', his son Martin did make additions to the text. Where these occur they have been highlighted and hand-writing samples have enabled the Editor to distinguish between the writing of Nathaniel and his son.[1]

The father's 26 sections appear broken down by subject matter but interspersed among his father's

---

[1] Martin Bladen's hand-writing: Cambridge University Library, Ch(H) Corr/1148; Cholmondeley Houghton Collection, letter dated 14th July 1724. Letter from Martin Bladen to Sir Robert Walpole. Nathaniel Bladen's hand-writing: Yorkshire Archaeological Society, MS614, letters dated 1715 between Frances Hammond (née Bladen) and her father Nathaniel

writings, on a few verso pages, there are several pages written by Martin. These contain an ad-hoc collection of poems, anagrams, memorable quotations and parables which, for the purpose of this work, have been shown separately at the rear on pages 81-85.

Martin Bladen's additions to the 'Advice' were probably done not too long after he received the manuscript from his father.[1]

After Westminster School, Martin went into the army where he served under Marlborough in the Low Countries during the War of the Spanish Succession, he later served as aide-de-camp to the Earl of Galway and became Colonel of a regiment in Spain.

After he left the army, Martin went into politics having two parliamentary seats in Ireland and several in England. He was a close friend of Sir Robert Walpole, by whose patronage he secured the appointment of Chief Secretary to the Lords Justices in Ireland before being appointed Lord Commissioner for Trade and Plantations. This was a post he held for the remainder of his days.

NOTES: Previously, only a précis of 'Advice to a Son' has appeared in the Editor's publications 'Martin Bladen: A Biography' and 'Early Yorkshire Bladens'. In the present full version, grammar,

---

[1] Martin Bladen: A Biography by Karen Proudler, 2015

punctuation and spelling have been reproduced largely as Nathaniel and Martin Bladen left them. However, generally the early part of the 'Advice' had an over-abundance of punctuation whilst the latter part had hardly any, so the Editor has introduced a small amount of punctuation towards the end of the manuscript sufficient only to make the text more readable. In respect of passages in Latin, these are entirely the author's and there has been no attempt to assess the accuracy of translations where there are any, these too are the author's work.

The original script was broken into 26 Sections but there were no headings, these were added by the Editor though not all content within these sections stays strictly on topic. The language is, for the most part, rhetorical, as if the father was speaking out loud to his young child. Nathaniel used terse sentences which he probably spent considerable time composing; as if he gave subjects immense thought but then sought to compact the result of his perceived wisdom into the fewest possible words, resulting in statements that are compacted, intense and thought-provoking. Almost every sentence, therefore, is a paragraph in itself and demands slow reading.

From the ultimate destination of Bladen's 'Advice to a Son' being in America, it can be speculated what became of Nathaniel's essay after his son took receipt of it. Clearly Martin added to it perhaps with the intention of passing it on to his own son. In the event Martin's heir was a daughter but he did become guardian to two nephews: Thomas Bladen and Edward Hawke. Thomas Bladen was the son of Martin's older brother who remained in Maryland and died there and, as Martin was charged with the care of Thomas after his father William's death, it seems highly likely that Martin passed on the 'Advice' to him. Thomas, who had been sent to England for his education when only 14 years old, returned to America many years later. He probably took the 'Advice' with him and, eventually, the essay came into the hands of the Folger Shakespeare who preserve the original to this day.

If it were not for the Folger purchasing Bladen's 'Advice' back in 1960 from the Seven Gables Antiquarian Bookshop in New York, it would have been just another book that disappeared in the course of history.

'Advice to a Son' was more than just advice to a young man about to go off for his education, it was a father's memorial: the place where the son could always seek refuge in the future for his father's direction and advice, advice which was borne of long, hard experience.

ADVICE TO A SON

Caste & Caute [*Chaste and Cautious*]

Son,

I know you are ingenious & industrious, the conjunction of two such planets in your youth doth p[re]sage much good to you.

You are now entring upon the theatre of the World where every one must act his p[ar]t, which p[ar]t you shall act I know not; but if it be your fortune to act that of a Beggar, doe it with as much grace & comelynesse as you can.[1]

Section 1 - Studies

Never p[er]plex your head with the scholars, whether a Myriad of Angells can dance the unique peece upon the point of a needle.

Nor spend pretious time in the finding out the proportion between a Cylinder & the Sphere, tho' the invention highly pleased Archimedes.[2]

---

[1] Nathaniel's language paraphrases Shakespeare here: "A Stage where every man must play a part" (Merchant of Venice), or, "All the world's a stage and all the men and women merely players" (As you Like It)
[2] Ancient Greek Mathematician

Neither will it become you to quarrell the orthography[1] of a word & whether we should write falix or felix.

It wil be an instance of great prudence in you, to study things which may be of solid use, & come home to business; the whole point of learning is infested with frivolous disputations, & vane impostures.

I must confess ye speculations of the metaphysicks (which are nothing but the needless work of curious braines) are exceeding pleasant; but pleasure without profit is a flower without a root.

And all the Philosophy in Aristotle & Plato,[2] or the Sublime theorems of the Scholar will not pay one debt.

Add to your own stores from observacion & experiences; a way of learning as far beyond that which is got by precept as the knowledge of a Traveller exceeds that which is got by a Mapp.

The whole universe is your library, conversations living studyes and observances your best Tutors.

The new world of experiments is left to your discovery of posterity; but it hath ever been your unhappy fate (which is great pitye) of new inventtions to be undervalued, witnesse that excellent

[1] Spelling of words
[2] Greek Philosophers Aristotle and Plato

discovery of Collumbus, with the great neglect he underwent before & after it.

But let nothing discourage you, worth is ever at home & carrieth its owne welcome with it; your own vertue, will enable you, and a gallant spirit will make you Caesar's kinsman.

Section 2 - Religion

Link not y'rselfe with any people or designe but with all Christians in Communion. For you will find it true in some p[er]sons that Maxima pars studiorus est studio partied. [The largest part of the study is studied parties].

For myselfe I wish you Christian World unity in your few fundamentalls, which are necessary; liberty in things indifferent & Charity in all things.

I know there are many things obtruded upon the World as Oracles of heaven, which they are but the accustomed cheats & delusions of imposters.

But wise men cannot be content to be abused with umbrages, nor is the world any longer to be entertained with dark Lanthornes [lanterns] since God hath sayd fiat lux ("let there be light": Genesis 1:3).

I must confesse I have not faith enough myselfe to swallow camells, nor can I p'swaid my reason to become a dromedary[1] to bear the whole luggage of Tradition, or the importunes of the Alcharan.

That religion to me seems best which is most Rationale, especially if we consider how much of interest & the strong impressions of Education, there is in that which many call Religion.

I do not speak this that you should try the Articles of the Creed by the touchstone of Aristotle. Be content with a single faith in God, the comforts of a good life, & the hopes of a better upon true Repentance & take the rest upon the authority of the Church.

In things necessary goe along with the Ancient Church, in things indifferent with the present.

Though you have some oppinions & notions of your own, yet yield (as your Orbs do) for the order of your universe, to the great will of the Church.

Let not your faith, which ought to stand firm upon a sure foundation lean too hard, on a well painted, yet rotten post.

If in scripture some points are left unto us lesse clear & positive, be content, it is that Christians might have where with to exercise humility in themselves, & charity towards others.

If you designe to make yourselfe happy, look to your thoughts before they come to be desires; & entertain no thoughts which may blush in words.

---

[1] Dromedary is an Arabian camel

Be assured he hath no serious belief of God or of the world to come who dares be wicked.

Instead of a Catorset before you, a God whose ey[e] is always upon you; & therefore keep your ey[e] always upon him.

Fear to do anything against that God thou lovest, & then thou wilt not love to do anything ag[ain]st that God thou fearest; let your prayers be as fervent as your wants & your thanksgivings as your blessings & deliverances.

In the morning think what you have to doe for which ask God's blessing; at night think what you have done for which you must ask his pardon.

Never write letters & desire your correspond-dents to burne them; but assure yourselfe whatever you write, which you would not have known, shall ever by those persons to whom you entrusted them as for whose service you exposed yourselfe, be one day produced to destroy you. Believe this truth from him that hath experienced it himselfe and seen it so fall out to many others. - LD, Ly F.[1]

In negotiating between great persons let it be your prudent care by fair representations of matters to compose things with amity rather than inflame the quarrel; for they will deny all they have sayd making themselves friends at your charge and grind you between two millstones.

---

[1] This could be a reference to Lord Danby and Lady Fairfax

And not a few have been thus undone.

Take an exact account of your life; be not afraid to look upon your score, but fearfull to encrease it, to despair becaus a man is sinfull is to be wors becaus he hath been bad.

In all your actions aim at excellency; that man will fail at last who allowes himself, one sinfull thought.

And he that dares sometime to be wicked for his advantage wilbe always so, if his interest require it.

Make even with heaven by Repentance at the end of every day, & so you shall have but one day to repent of before your death.

Section 3 - King

Next your duty to God I require ye that you preserve your loyalty to your King, never sell honor to purchase the brand of a trator.

A secure & happy subjection is more to be esteemed than a dangerous & factious liberty.

Government is the greatest security of freedome; for as obedience in subjects is the Princes strength; so is the same their owne safety, therefore they who weaken the Soveragne power, infring their own security.

Never suffer the dignity of his p[er]son to be slurred; for the most effectuall method of disobedience is first to sully the glory of his p[er]son & then to overthrow his power.

As Rebellion is a weed of hasty growth, so it will decay as suddainly, & that knot which is united in Treachery, will easily be dissolved by jealousys.

Great crimes are full of fears, delays & frequent chang of councells, & that which in the p'jection seemed full of its reward, when it comes to action looks big with danger.

And let me tell you your ends of the comon people, if nuzled up in a factious liberty, are much different from the designs of sovraigne Princes.

Submission to your Prince is your duty & confidence in his goodnesse will be your prudence.

Let no pretence of conscience render you disobedient to his Comands, for obedience to your Prince is p[ar]t of your duty towards God.

And Conscience is not your Ruler but your guide, & so far onely can conscience justify your actions, as it is selfe justifyed by God in his Sacred word.

Remember always that Kings have quick ears, & long hands, they catch affar off & their blowes are dangerous.

Section 4 - Conversation

Let your conversation be with those by whome you may accomplish yourselfe best, for vertue never returnes with so rich a Cargo as when it sets saile from such Continents; Company like climats alter Complexions.

Keep company with p'sons rather above than below yourselfe, for Gold in the same pocket with Silver, looses both colour & weight.

Retein your own vertues, & by imitation naturalize other mens; but let none be copyes to you longer than they agree with your originall; study to gain respect not by little observances but by a constant fair carriage.

Hear no ill of a friend nor speak no ill of an enemy; believe not all you hear, nor speak all you believe.

Never comend any p'son to his face but to others, to creat in them a good oppinion of him: disparag no man behind his back; but to himselfe, to work a reformacion in him of his fault.

Over great commendations and laudatives of any p'son doe not suite with prudence, for is a sort of detraction from those with whom you converse and it will expresse arrogance in you; for he that comends another would have him esteemed on his judgm't.

Section 5 - Behaviour

Nothing will gain you more reputation with the pe[o]ple than a serene humble deportm't & an equall temper.

A rude & morose behaviour in conversation, is as absurd as the forme of a round quadrangle in the mathematicks.

Civility is a debt you owe to mankind, civill language, & good behaviour wilbe like p[er]petuall letters comendatory & procure you good offices wherever ye come.

Let your behaviour like your garment be neither too streight, nor too loos but becoming.

In conversation avoyd idle jeasts, vain complem'ts & long digressing discourses: the one being crepitus ingeni[1] the other but verball idolatry, vertue like a stone ever best when plain set.

By tryfles are the qualityes of men as well disclosed as by great actions; becaus in matters of importance they comonly temporize and strayne themselves; but in lesser things they follow the current of their own natures.

You will meet with many p'sons (as I myselfe have done) which are wise in picture & exceeding formall, but they are so far from resolving of Riddles with Oedipus that they are more Riddles themselves.

---

[1] Chattering talent

Of those you must have a care for, a pedant & a formalist are two dangerous animals; but to the Solons and Heroes of your age, out of duty pay them an honorable regard & memory.

If you meet with a p'son subject to infirmityes never deride him; but blesse God you have no occasion to blush or grieve for them in yourselfe.

Section 6 - Discretion

Be not futile & over-talkative, that is the fools Paradise; but a wise mans Purgatory: it doth expresse a great weaknesse in you & doth imply a believing that others are affected with the same vanity.

Speak well or say nothing so that if others be not better by your sylence they may not be worse by your discourse.

By your sylence you have this advantage, you observe other mens follyes & conceal your own: and he discovers his abilities most that least discovers himselfe, not that I would have you sullenly reserved, that is a symptome of ill nature & uneasy to all society.

But let your discourse be solid, not like a ship that carryes more saile than ballast.

There is no man that speaketh; but if you be wise you may gain from him, & none that is sylent if ye have not a care, but you many lose by him, if ye must speak it wilbe prudence in you ever to speak last, & so you will be master of others strength instead of discovering your own weaknesse.

Reservednesse will be your best security, & slownesse of belief the best sinew of wisdom; never impart that to a friend which may impower him to be your enemy (your servants, which usually prove the worst of enemyes, & often like Actaeon[1] dogs devour their m[aste]rs); you may admit into your bedchamber but never into your closett.

A secret, like a Crown, is no estate to be made over in trust, to whomsoever you comit it, you doe but enable him to undoe you, & you must purchase his secrecy at his own price; therefore let me advise you ever to carry two eyes about you, the one of warinesse upon yourselfe and the other of observacion upon other men.

Consider how precarious & unhappy your life & fortune wilbe which depends upon so slender a thread as another's pleasure.

Never trust twice where you have [been] deceived once.

---

[1] Actaeon, in Greek Mythology was transformed into a stag and killed by his own dogs

Section 7 - Humility

Bee not magisterialle or too affirmative in any assertion for the bould maintaining of any argum't doth conclud ag[ain]st your own civill behaviour; modesty in your discours will give a lustre to trueth & an excuse to your error.

If you desire to know how short your understanding is in things above you, consider how little you know of yourselfe: what your soul is, of what members your body is inwardly compacted, and what is the use of every bone, vein, artery and sinew, which no man understandeth as Gallen[1] himself confesseth.

I pay much reverence to the humility of Plato, Democritus, Anaxagoras, Empedocles[2] & all the new Academicks who possitively maintain that nothing in the world could be certainly known.

And Socrates[3] was by the Oracle adjudged the wisest man living because he was wont to say (I know only this) I know nothing; yet Archelaus[4] was of oppinion that not so much as that could be known which Socrates said he knew, that he knew nothing.

---

[1] Galen, AD 129-c200, Galen of Pergamon. Greek Physician and Philosopher of the Roman Empire
[2] Plato, Democritus, Anaxagoras and Empedocle were all Greek Philosophers
[3] Socrates, 470-399 BC, Greek Philosopher
[4] Archelaus (pupil of Anaxagoras) Ancient Greek Philosopher

Section 8 - Reputation

Be studious to p'serve your Reputation, if that be once lost you are like a cancell'd writing of no value, & at best you doe but survive your owne funeralls, for Reputation like a glass once cract, will ever be crasy, it will beget a contempt of you, & contempt like the Planet Saturn hath first an evill aspect & then a destroying influence.

A noble Reputation is a great Inheritance, it begetteth oppinion which ruleth the world. Oppinion riches, Riches honour.

But, howsoever, be carefull to keep up the Reputacion of your parts & vertue to the vulgar; for it will be more advantage to you to be accounted vertuous & learned by the Ignorant, than Ignorant by the Learned; for the Ignorant are many but the Learned are few.

It was a principle in Julius Caesar not to be eminent amongst the Magnificos, but to be chief amongst Inferiors.

Section 9 - Modesty

Never magnify yourselfe, or boast of your great actions; that is pedantry and as in fa[u]lconry, so take it for a truth, that those of the weakest wing are comonly ye higher flyers.

Make not yourselfe a body of Christalle that all men may look through you (but, as wise men ought to doe) be like Coffers with double bottoms, which no others look into being opened they see not all that they hould at once.

Let your discourse of others be fair; speak no ill of any; if ye do it in his absence 'tis the prop'ty of a Coward to stab a man behind his back, if it to his face you act as an affront to the scandal; every man looks upon his owne vertues & morrils through the great end of the glasse & upon other mens invers & thinks he deserves better than he does, therefore you cannot oblige mankind more than to speak well of them: man is the greatest humorist & flatterer of himselfe in the world.

No men are so ready to speak ille of others as they who deserve worse themselves; yet I have so much charity for them, that many times they doe not censure & condemne others, so much out of a principle of malice as thereby to gain a reputation (as they think) of being vertuous & just themselves.

Disoblige none, for there is no p'son so despicable but it may be in his power to be your best friend or worst enemy: if you do courtesye to 100 men & disoblige but one, that one shalbe more active to your ruine, than all the others shalbe to serve you, therefore if you will gain respect, turne userer & make all men enter into obligacions to you; The world is a shop of tools of which the wise man onely is the Master.

Section 10 - Passion

Never be so below yourselfe as to let any passion be above you: be assured when passion enters in at the foregate, wisdome goes out at the postern.

He that comands himself, comands the world too; & the more authority you have over others, the more comand you ought to have over yourselfe.

Set bounds to your zeal by discretion, to error by truth, to division by charity, to passion by reason.

I cannot chuse but admire the temper of that Persian who in his fury thretned the Tempest & whipt the seas.

It is a sorrow to me to see a passionate man scourge himselfe with his own scorpions and in the middst of his innocent contends fondly to give himself unnecessary alarms, be you like the Baltick or the Caspian Seas which neither ebb nor flow but enjoy a p'petual tranquillity.

Never have to doe with any man in his passion, for men are most contrary to iron worst to be wrought upon when they are hot.

It is more prudence to pass by trivial offences, than to quarrell for them; by the last ye are even with your adversary but by ye first above him.

It was a maxim worthy of Caesar's gallantry, 'nex infere nexe ppeti'. If you have an injury done you, you do your adversary too much hon[ou]r to take notice of it & think too meanly of yourselfe if you reveng it; let me advise you to dissemble an injury which you have not power to reveng it, & generously forgive it which you have the means to do it.

It is a noble way of Reveng to forget & scorne injuryes. Louis ye 12th of France, being advised by som of his Councell to punish such as were Enemyes to him, which he was Duke of Orléans, answered like a Prince that it did not suite with the glory of a King of France to revenge the injuries done the Duke of Orléans.

If you be displeased with every peccadillo you will become habitually frowned: learn patience by observing the inconvenience of impationce in other men.

I speak not this to you that I would have you without sence for 'pecora il Lupo la mangia', he that make himselfe a sheep shall be devoured by ye wolf.

I shall comend to your practice that excellent precept of Pythagoras, 'nil tarpe comittas neque cora alys neq leud, maxime uno verere leipsed'.

And believe it, a good man will blush as much to commit a sin in a wildernesse as upon a theatre: the lesser the occasion of sin the greater the nature of it, & to justify a fault is a greater crime than to fall into it; & let me tell you sin is masculine & begetts the like in others & many times like venome it infects the blood when the viper is dead which gave the wound; therefore take care that the bright lustre of your vertues may enlighten your whole sphere wherein you move.

I would not have any like a sundyall in the grave of noblese, or like the man before an Almanack placed amongst the signs to be wondred at.

As to acts of charity & vertue, let not your heart be a narrow island but a large continent: be your own almoner & dispose of your own charity; but as to favo'r & kindnesses imitate your wise husband-men who when they sow their ground do not sow all their seed in one place, but scatter and believe me small & comon courtesyes do more oblige than great favours, and when others are made pore by oppression, make you as many beggers as you can by your bounty.

And he that designs to gain all interest must make all interests gainers.

Section 11 - Friends

Out of your acquaintances choos familiars & amongst those pick friends.

But let me advise you never to make a Coward your friend, nor a drunkard your privy Counsells for the one upon the approach of the least danger will deserte you & the other will discover all your secretts; both dangerous to human society.

Friendship is a sacred thing & deserves our dearest acknowledgement & a friend is a great comfort in solitude, an excellent assistant in business & the best protection against injuryes.

Therefore I cannot but hug the resolucion of that Philosopher who, when he was dying, ordered his friends to be inventoried amongst his goods.

A friend like a glass will best discover to you your own defects.

But never purchase friends by guifts, for if you was to give, they will was to love.

Love is built upon the union of minds, not the bribery of guifts, & the more you give, the fewer friends you will have.

An enemy is better recovered by kindnesses then a friend assured: make no man your friend twice, except the rupture was by your own mistake, & you have don penance for it.

When you have made choice of your friend, express all civility to him; yet in prudence I doe advise you to look upon your present friend as your future enemy.

I confess myselfe a citizen of the world, & have such an aversion to any think that is unkind, that I look upon an injury don to another as don to myselfe.

And many times when I have heard that my friend was dead I have deluged mine eyes with tears & could as passionately have wept over his sacred tomb as that Grecian Matron did for the loss of her Mother, but when I considered, it was more kindnesse in me than prudence; for I might as reasonably have wept that my friend was born no sooner as that he should live no longer.

Section 12 - Money

Study not onely to preserve your estate, but justly to encrease it; money is the byre of fortune & Lord Paramount of the world.

Riches are power, the keyes to greatnesse & makes the access to hon[ou]r more easy and open.

It is storied that a noble man of Venice made his address to Cosimo de Medici, Duke of Florence & signified to him that he understood his highness had the Philosophers Stone & desired to see it.

It is true, sayd the Duke, but my elixor is this: never to doe that by another which I can doe myselfe, nor to do that tomorrow as I can doe today, never to neglect the least things. The Venetian thankt his highness, took his leave of him & by the observacion hereof became the wisest & richest man in Venice. If your purpose is to be rich and wise study this Elixor.

I know the generous mind least regards money, & when they have it not none want it more; and the most excell't p[er]son w[ith]out an estate is like a ship well rigged but cannot sayl for want of wind.

If your estate be but small, come seldome into company, but when you doe let your money go friely. Have a care you do not imitate his fortune who, labouring to boy up a sunk ship of another, bulged his own vessell.

I have read there was a goddesse fastned to an oak in a grove who for a long time had many Worshippers; but when the tree was ready to fall, none would come within the shaddow of her statue: he that supports a falling wall courts his own monum't.

Love & respect are rarely found in lost fortunes, & adversity seldom meets with the returns of friendship.

The World hath no kindnesse nor affection but interest & though you have many p'sons allyed to you, yet you will find them most kind to their own interest.

And believe it, Charity though a Saint, is yet without an altar in the world.

You will meet with many men that have much of the heliotrope in them, which open in the sunshine of prosperity, but towards the night of adversity, or in stormy seasons, shut & contract themselves.

Section 13 - Riches

I am not by my constellation destined to be rich, neither do I much care for the more a man hath the more he wanteth.

And Riches were to be sought after above all things, if they brought content, as well as content brings them; if they be for reall uses, then it followeth, he who hath not need of so many things as another, is richest of the two and be assured he who needeth least is most like God.

Crassus accounted him a rich man who had an Estate to manetayne an army but, believe me, he that hath an estate to keep an army, had need have an army to keep his Estate.

Get all the possessions of the Earth, yet if you measure your own shaddow (as Archidamus told Philipp of Macedon) he should not find it longer than before.

The Rich man liveth happily so long as he useth his riches temperately, & the poor man that patiently endures his wants is rich enough.

Methinks when I see a poor man drink out of his hand I could, with Diogenus,[1] throw away my dish. And many times, wish with Crassus, that the stones were bread, as well as the water drink, that we might have a certain provision by nature.

---

[1] Diogenus, Greek Philosopher and cynic

To have no estate and not to want; to want & not desire; to take the changes of the world & without any change in yourselfe are excellent qualifications of which to get to be Master.

Abundances is a trouble, honour a burthen, advancem't dangerous; but competency is a blessing: I have all I desire if I have as much as I want, & I have as much as the most if I have as much as keeps me.

Of all p'sons, I look upon them to be happy who have their estates in their own hands, (I mean Labourers), for as they never gain much, so their wants are never great.

However let me advise you to make use of your estate while you live, for when you dye you shall leave it to the greatest enemyes you have, who wished your death when you were living. And when you are dead you are no more concerned in that you shall leave behind you than you were before you were born in what was then; therefore get well to live, & then study to live well.

Section 14 - The Law

If you designe to yourselfe happyness and an improvement of your estate, let me advise you to avoid suits in law.

If you engage in any, you put yourselfe into a hous of correction where you must punch stoutly to pay your fees.

If your case shall goe for you there are those that will tell you that victory is a fair game, but you must give them leave to decide the stakes.

If it be your misfortune to engage in any, have a care of a rich fool, for there is nothing more dangerous as to mischiefe as a rich, obstinate fool in the hands of a cunning knave.

Two lawy'rs, who very passionately pleaded their clyents caus to their great satisfaction, when the case was over the lawyers came out of court & hugged each other. The Clyents much admireing their behaviour, one of the Clyents asked his lawyer how they could be friends so soon. Hush man, says the lawyer, we were never foes, for we lawyers are like a pair of sheers, if you open them & then put them down, they seem to cut one another, but they cut only that which was between them.

You remember the apologie of the vulture sitting upon a tree to see the lyon & the bear fight & to make prey of each of them which fell first, have a care you doe not make the morrall.

I speak not this to reflect upon that hon'able profession to which I shall ever pay the greatest tribute of my services & I know there are many excellent p'sons towards the Law, if it be your fortune to meet with them.

But, you will be sure at every mercato[1] in the country to find Fairly Elves and little spirits with hawking bags and snapsacks by their sides, wherein they have their familiars, some in green coats, others with yellow vests which they send forth to the disquiet of good men, as Eolus [Aeolus][2] did the winds he had gott into his bottle, to the disturbance of the world: certainly those Elves are much of the nature with you. And very good for themselves, but exceeding punctilious in the garden of a Common-wealth.

If ever you should fly to those for succour as the sheep doe to bushes in a storm, you wilbe sure to leave a good p[ar]t of your coat behind you; these, like a quartan ague,[3] will never leave you as long as any humour is left in you, & if you have need to make use of them they will stir no more without their fee than a hawk without a lure.

My advice to you is that you seriously apply yourself in the study of the Laws of this nation, being the most excellent for their justice & wisdome. If not to practice the Law, yet to gain so much knowledge therein as to defend yourselfe & estate from the Robin good-fellons of it.

If you be not so disposed you must lay up one third p[ar]t of your Revenue to pr'serve your other two, or els it will be assuredly undone.

---

[1] Market
[2] Aeolus, from Greek Mythology: the Keeper of the Winds
[3] Quartan ague returns every four days

Section 15 - Law Suits

Next, suites in law which are but 'iactus alea'.[1] Avoyd gameing; it hath no satisfaction in it, besides the sordid coveting of that which is anothers, or upon legality of that which is your own.

Consider what a vanity it is to cast a dye whether your estate shall be your own or not: if you have not a care I can tell you that without an augure[2] tell you what wilbe your fate this, like a quicksand, will swallow you up in a moment & goods which are so gotten are like pyramids of snow, which melt away & are dissolved, with the same ill husbandry they were begotten.

Section 16 - Marriage

There is one step more to make your life comfortable, & to advance your fortune; & that is well to dispose of yourselfe in marriage, which is certainly a business which requires your grave consideracion.

---

[1] 'Alea iacta est' - "the die is cast". Words spoken by Julius Caesar in 49 BC as he crossed the River Rubicon with his army

[2] In Ancient Rome, an Augur was a religious officer who interpreted divine desires from natural signs

Ride not post for your match, if you doe you may, in the period of your journey, take sorrow for your Inn and make repentance your Host.

Choos rather to make the world happy than numerous. [Recepient/son, Martin Bladen, inserted these words in bold/italic].

Prefer in marriage a vertuous woman, a Celebrated Beauty like a fair, will draw chapmen[1] from all p[a]rts.

Never marry so much for a great Living as a good life; yet a fare wife without a portion is like a brave hous without furniture; you may please yourselfe with the prospect, but there is nothing within to keep you warme.

Be sure you love her person better than her estate: for he who marrieth where he doth not love will be sure to love where he doth not marry.

Remember there is a great difference between a portion & a fortune with your wife; if she be not vertuous let her portion be never so great, she is no fortune to you.

Me thinks the zeal of that prize did trespass upon his discretion, to him at a wedding sermon, he much comended marriage but compared the woman to a grave.

---

[1] Chapmen/pedlars

For an early grave (saith he) hath an hie-jact, so soon you come to marry; hie-jact the wisdom of Solomon, hie-jact the Valor of David, hie-jact ye strength of Sampson & c.

I must confess I ever had a noble affection for ye excellent sex, as a great instrument of good and the pretinesse of society, & ever thought that of all follyes in man, there is none more excusable than that of Love; but I find by myselfe that that Passion will grow ould & wear out in time.

Section 17 - Action

When you come upon the stage of action, as it is your duty, so it wilbe your glory to deal justly & honestly with all p'sons.

Clear & round dealing is the honour of mans nature: hate nothing but what is dishonest, fear nothing but what is ignoble & love nothing but what is just & hon[oura]ble.

To stoop to any sordid, low action is to imitate the kite, which flyeth high in the aire, yet vouchsafeth to condiscend to carrion on upon the ground.

Injure none for by so doing you teach others the way to injure you.

Innocence wilbe your best guard & your integrity wilbe a coat of mail to you.

Section 18 - Honesty

It is less difficult & more safe to keep your way of honesty & integrity than to turn from it, yet comonly our passions lead us.

And be assured he that in any one affair relinquished honesty, banishes all shame in succeeding actions & certainly no view covereth a man with so much shame as to be found false or unjust.

Keep touch in lesser matters not to deceive in greater, but the better to dispose yourselfe to p'forme things of weight & moment: a promise is a just debt which you must take care to pay, for hon'r and honesty are your security & hostages.

Borrow before you have need & pay before the day promised, it will gain you credit. Breaking your faith may gain you riches, but never get you glory.

It was well said by Mr Georgius, a French Capitain who, haveing burnt many of the churches of ye Spaniards in Florida & being asked why he did so, answered they who had no faith needed no Churches.

Before you act, it is prudence soberly to consider; for after action you cannot recorde without dishonesty.

Take the advice of some prudent friend, for he that wilbe his own counsell shall be sure to have a fool for his Clyent.

Resolutions are ye moulds wherein actions are cast, if they be taken with ever much hast or too much affection seldom doe they receive good successe.

When you have fully resolved which course to take in any action, you must not afterwards Repent, or fear any difficulty, for such things will lessen the gallantry of your minde.

And although some difficultyes happen to arise, yet you must believe that every other cours wold have been accompanyed with the same or greater impediments; yet many times it is more prudence to follow the directions of a pr'sent good fortune than the first resolucions.

In the conduct of affairs, you may show a brave spirit in going on, but your wisdom will most appear in securing your Retreit, & how to come off, for there is so great uncertainty in all humane affairs that, that course to me seemes best which hath most passages out of it.

Section 19 - Business

In business be active, sylent & industrious, for many men of large abilityes relying wholy upon their wits, & neglecting the use of ordinary means, suffer others lesse able but more active & industrious to goe beyond them.

Diligent action is a fair fortune & industry a good Estate. Slothnesse doth as insencibly waste a man as industry doth improve him.

If success in businesse does not at first answer your expectation, let no fumes of melancholy possess you, use other expedients & addresses, for he that constantly makes head against the assaults shalbe sure to be victorious & attaine his ends. 'Tu no ced matis sed contra audentior ito' (Every thing hath two handles, if the one proves hot & not to be touched you may take the other that is more temperate).

When a business may turne to disadvantage it will be your wisdome to temporize & delay & get what time you can by differring; becaus time may occasion some accident which may remove the danger.

But if it be for your advantage, delayes are dangerous & you must act with secrecy & clarity, the two wheels upon which all great actions move.

To spend that time in a grave gaze upon Businesse which might serve for a speedy dispatch thereof, is to imitate the Musician who spent so much time in tuning his instrument that he had no time left to exercise his musick.

If the matter you undertake be doubtfull, warrant your own diligence, but keep no offer of assurance to warrant the success; remember ye Italian make it p[ar]t of the character of an

Englishman when he undertaketh any thing p'sently he sayeth he warrant you, but when he misseth of his undertaking he says who would have thought it.

However use circumspection in all your actions for he who intendeth what he doth is most likely to do what he intends; halfe doing in any thing is worse than no doing & a middle course in case of extremity is ever the worst.

It was excell't advice of Tiberius Caesar 'non committal caput revid noq', follow safe courses by reason rather than happy by chance.

Yet somethings must be ventured, & many things which exceed the prudence of man, are often by fortune disposed to the best.

Certain it is that he who will comit nothing to fortune, nor undertake any enterprize whose event appeareth not infallible escape many dangers by his wary conduct but fails of as many successes by his inactive fearfulenesse.

It will be great prudence in you rightly to take hold an opportunityes or, for opportunity admitts of no after game, and those that have lost their first hopes, any thing that is future seems best.

In management of affairs stand not upon nicetyes & punctillios of honour, but by fair compliance, gain your ends, heat & precipitancy is fatall to all businesse; a sober patience & a wise condisencion doe many times effect that which rashness & choler [colour] certainly ruine & undo.

If you are to negotiate a matter with any p[er]son, observe his tone (& as far as prudence and discretion will give leave) comply with his humour, & so you shall the better effect your designe.

Converse with all men as Christians but if you have to doe with any p'sons look upon born as unjust (its severe, but it wilbe your greatest safety for distrust & slownesse in belief are your chief sinews of wisdome) if he proves otherwise he does but faile your expectation, for believe me (& I have found it to my cost) nothing will undo you more than to rely too much upon the honesty of other men.

And if possible, order your affairs so that he performs first; when that is done, if you be deceived, you may thank yourselfe.

If at any time you be overmuch pressed to doe anything hastily, be carefull, fraud & deceipt are ever in hast, diffidence is the right ey[e] of prudence; 'Cavenda tutus' [Safe by taking care].

In all great actions take many, if you pleas, to your assistance, but few to your trust.

When you have a p[re]sent good in prospect which may turne to advantage, decline it not by the importunity of any, if you doe you will make work for repentance: let the businesse of the world be your circumference; but yourselfe the centre.

If you meet with a p[er]son more complacent & officious to you than usuall, have a care for he hath some designe upon you & he either hath or doth intend to deceive you.

Section 20 - Deception

Keep an exact dyary of all your actions and of your most memorable passages you hear or meet with.

And if in the conduct of your affairs you have been deceived by others or have comitted any error yourselfe, it will be discretion in you to note the same & your design, & your modas or expedients to repair it, for it will make you more prudent & wary for the future.

For let me tell you, no man is truely wise but he who hath been deceived, & your owne errors will teach you more prudence than the grave precepts & examples of others.

Let all your observacions & remarques be comitted to writing, every night before you sleep, & so in a short time you will have a dictionary of your prudence & experience of your own making.

It wilbe exceeding pleasant to you to read and a great advantage to build you up to such a height of knowledge more in one year than otherwise you would have gained in many. And wise men begin not to be content to inhabit the world onely, but to understand it also.

Section 21 - Complacency

It will be great prudence in you well to study the art of complacency, certainly an act of excellent use in your conduct of affairs.

For there are so many circumstances in your way to an estate, or greatnesse, that a morose or pre-emptory man rarely attaineith either.

Make sail whilst the wind blowes, follow the current whilst and where the stream is strongest, for if fortune be followed as you first doth fall out, the rest will comonly follow.

Never violently oppose yourself against the torrent of the times you live in, thereby to hazard your fame or fortune, but by fair complyance attaine your safety.

Plato compares a wise man to a good gamester who doth accomodate his play to the chances of the Day, so should a wise man accomodate the cours of his life to the occasions which often require new deliberations.

Be not singular, but observe the humor & genious of the times, you must imitate M. Porcius Cato[1] who was of such a temper that he could fashion himselfe to all occasions, as if he were never out of his Element; a wise Pilote always turns his sailes to the winds.

---

[1] Marcus Porcius Cato c234-149 BC, Roman Senator (Cato the Elder)

When the c[h]ameleon cannot change culler with the air he lives in, must then the c[h]ameleon be content to live onely on the air.

He that in a wicked age will endeavour to do that which ought to be done, or study to be truly vertuous and just (which I wish you ever to be), will thereby hazard his fortune & his safety & believe me more men are undone for their vertue than for their vices, & a good life is more suspected than a bad.

Theodorus the Patriarch[1] was scoffed at by the Gretian Court as an antick for using goodness, when it was out of fashion, and adjudged imprudent for being vertuous by himselfe.

In Elder story, it passed for an Oracle of Prudence that honesty is the best policy, but in modern practice you will find that politics is the best honesty.

Vertue & integrity, when men were good and innocent, were great securityes, but in a depraved estate they are but as traps to ensnare those that doe possess them.

But if it shall be your infelicity to live in bad times, I hope you may be better for them by an antiperistatis. If the times be perillous you must, as a discrete pilote, play with the waves which may endanger you & by giving way thereto avoyd the

---

[1] Theodorus I, Patriarch of Alexandria (607-609) A.D.

hazard; so the tempest may slack but not render your safely.

In all factions carry yourself with moderation, & by that means you may make use of all p'tyes.

But in popullar commotions, if you stand neutrall, you will be sure to run your fortune of the batt to be pockt by the birds & bitten by the mass.

If any signall infelicity fall upon you, the only way is not to sit still but resolve upon action, for so long as nothing is don the same accidents which caused your misfortune remaine, & if you act something, you may deliver yourselfe, however you express a brave spirit that you durst attempt it.

But that which is out of your power, let it be out of your care; you may if you think fit give yourselfe much trouble, but leave God to governe the World as he himselfe pleases. If you will live comfortably, let God alone with his providence & men with their Rights.

Section 22 - Advancement

If you aim at advancem't be sure you have Jovem in Arca,[1] otherwise your flight to p'fermt wilbe but slow, without some golden feathers.

You must study to enworthy yourselfe into the fav'rite of some great p'son, upon whom you must

---

[1] Jovem - Jupiter, the Planet of Luck. Arca - Ark, or trunk

lean rather than upon your own vertues; if not you will be like a hop without a polle to ly upon the ground, to be trampled upon.

Though vertue be a Patent for honour and p'ferment & ought to be an encouragem't for worth, yet in the Epoch and acc[oun]t of times, we have observed that men of the greatest abilityes are, on designe, suppressed when they deal with p'sons of the best accomplishments: as the Birds in Plutarch did, who beat the Jay, lest in time she might prove an Eagle.

And it hath been the unhappy fate of many vertuous p'sons, who like the axe after it hath hewen out the hard timber, to be hanged up against the unregarded; or like a Topp which hath for a long time been scourged & run well, yet at last to be lodged up for a hobler.

But me thinks tis great pity to see the Curtain drawn between a vertuous p[er]son and preferment: nor can I with cander maintain that Injustice ought to be preferred to Justice; or that it is better to be a knave than a vertuous honest man.

But many times I am under such a paroxysms that I am almost induced to think that it is better to be fortunate than wise or just, & cannot but with Brutus cry out 'O virtus [te] colui ut rem, sed nomen inane!'[1]

---

[1] Te colui, virtus, ut rem: ast tu nomen inane es. (Yet the divine foundation is upon the rock)

Section 23 - Virtue

But let nothing disquiet you, a vertuous p'son will at one time or another be thought good for some thing, & a wise man will, once in an age, come in fashion.

I am much pleased with a remark of Themistocles[1] upon the Athenians who resembled himselfe to a plane tree; tho' leaves & boughs whereof men broke off in fair weather, but run under it for shelter in a storme.

You must know that honour and preferments are rarely the reward of vertue but the effort of pleasure or interest. Is it not strange to observe a p'son raised to the dignity of a Constable of France for haveing taught Magpies to fly at Sparrows.

To which Grandure do you think such another p'son as Domitian,[2] if he had lived in that Princes time, wold have advanced himselfe, who was so excellent at catching of flyes; but let honour be your merit, not your expectation; & attain to pr'ferm't not by winding stairs but by the scale of your own vertues, if you mis of it you must be content there is a reward for every thing of vertue.

Beware of ambition (that ever rides without Reines) lest you catch a fall for many men, like sealed doves, they study to rise higher & higher,

---

[1] Themistocles 524-449 B.C., Greek General, a supporter of the lower classes
[2] Domitian, 51-96 A.D., Roman Emperor

they know not whither; little considering that when they are mounted to ye solstar of their greatnesse, every step they set is paved with fate; and their fall how gentle soever will never suffer them to rise again.

That which a wise man hath to doe in this world is to make his life comfortable.

Satisfy yourselfe that it is the best living in the temperate zone; nor splendide, nor miserè. If heaven shall vouchsafe me such a blessing that I may enjoy a grote or molehill with content, I can with him in Lucian, look upon all the great kingdoms of the earth as so many birds neasts.

And I can, in such a territory, prune myself as much as Alexander did when he phansied the whole world to be one great city & his camp the castle of it.

And you will find by experience, the best looking-Glasse of Wisdom, that a private life is not onely more pleasant, but more happy that any princely state.

The tallest trees are ever weakest in the topps, & envy always aimed at the highest.

Those who have been bad, their own infelicity precipitates their fate; if good, their morils have been their ruine. If they have been fortunate abroad, they have been undone at home by fear & jealousyes. If unsuccessfull, the caprices of fortune are counted their miscarriages & their unhappiness esteemed their crimes.

Section 24 - Favourite

But if it be your fortune to rise, to become a favourite to a great p'son, as you may have some hopes in Eutopia, for I have heard men are advanced there for their merit & worth, you must understand there are many dores which open to p'ferm't but the Prince keeps the keys of them all.

Therefore be sure to study well your alphabet of his humour & observe his inclinations as your Astronomers do the Lord of your Ascendant, & the Mariners the North Star.

For great p'sons accompt these the wisest men that can best suite themselves to their humour &, usually, they extend their affections no farther than their own satisfaction. And to deal truly with you, the life of those who would wait upon great persons is nothing but the art of fencing; he that dither on the right or left side hits their humour; wins and p[ar]takes of their bounty but not he that useth much skills.

Therefore as Princes have arts to governe kingdoms, so favourites must have arts by which they may govern their Prince.

Desire not to monopolize his ear, for his misadventures will be imputed to you & what is well don wilbe ascribed to himselfe.

Too great services will be oversight and weaknesse in you; that merit to which reward may easily reach is ever best & safest.

Broadly to give an accompt of all your transactions is required, for he that feareth the touch is like gold that hath too great an alloy.

In doubtfull enterprises never give violent counsells; for that wilbe rather a testimony of your love than of your wisdom.

If the success be ill, it will assuredly be cast on you, & the good will not meet with a reward which may answer your hazard & danger.

Ever think those counsells best which have your greatest facility & security in them: counsells too finely spun are easily broken.

Profer safer counsells with reason, before rash ones, onely chance can make p[ro]sperous.

And always remember that good success issuing from bad counsell is more to be feared than calamity itselfe, for the one breeds foolish confidence, & the other teaches men to be wary.

It will be wisdome in you in great concernes not to rest in the dull Counsells of what is lawfull, but to p[ro]ceed to quick resolution of what is safe.

In all your deport[men]t be humble & of easy accesse, a favourite likes coine to which vertue may give ye strength but it is humility must give the weight.

A high fortune, like great buildings, must have low foundations.

Pride doth ill become any p[er]son, & though no man be thereby injured, yet every man is thereby offended & none can endure an excessive fortune any where so ill as in those who have been in an equall degree to themselves.

Be you minima in summe, like the Orient Stars; the higher they are, the lesser they appear: and why should you be proud?

Is it of honour, alas tis, 'bonum sino clari & sora'? It is like the rose which, in the evening makes its tomb of your tearlet, which in the morning was its cradle; to be proud of knowledge is to blind with light, to be proud of vertue is to poyson yourselfe with the antidote; to be proud of authority is to make your risk your downfall.

To be humble to superiors is duty, to equalls courtesy, to inferiors noblenesse, to all - safety and advantage.

Ever think goodness the best part of greatnesse, when honour & vertue are in conjunction, it is a noble aspect & Jupiter is Lord of that assent.

But greatness without goodness is like the Colossus of Rhodes,[1] not so much to be admired

---

[1] Colossus of Rhodes, statue in Rhodes 280 B.C., one of the seven Wonders of the Ancient World

for its workmanship as its huge bulk; therefore make goodnesse a support to greatnesse, like a Diamond sett in Gold.

Greatness may make your tombe but it is goodnesse must write the Epitaph.

Section 25 - Flattery

Give things their right Colour, not varnishing them over with a fals glosse. A flatterer is a dangerous fly insect, yet they often thrive and p'sper better than more worthy & brave men doe.

But I would advise you to have so much of your Persian Religion in you as to adore the Rising Sun: and observe this 'nominom tristem demistere', and when you cannot give men satisfaction in that they desire; entertain them with fair hopes. Denialls must be ushered in by civille usage, & tho' you cannot cure the sore, yet your prudence may abate the sence of it.

If you have any venturous designe in projection, its prudence before you come to action, sometimes to give things out on purpose, to see how they will take, & by that means you will discover the inclynations of the people you are to deal with, if it hath no fair reception p'sonally chock it, & make no further p[ro]gress.

If you desire the designs you labour may not prove abortive, do not assigne them a certain day of their birth but leave them to the naturall p[ro]ductions of fit times & occasions, like the curious artists in China, who temper the mould this day whereof a vessell may be made an hundred years hence.

If you have enemyes, as ye must expect many being great in your master's favour, the better to establish yourselfe, is privately to give out fals libells & reports tending to your own disgrace. Your enemies, like powder, will fire at the first touch, & discover themselves; and then you know what you have to doe. And to deal plainly with you, the greatnesse of one man is nothing but the ruine of others, & their weakness will be your strength.

Section 26 - Conclusion

If any Pasquills[1] or libells shall be vented against you by others, (as the most excellent p[er]sons many times are infested with them), its more prudence to bury them in their own ashes than by conflating them to ad[d] new flames, for libells neglected p[re]sently find a grave & perish.

But let me tell you, as fals rumours & libells are not always to be credited, so are they not always to be condemned, it being no lesse vain to fear all things, than dangerous to doubt of nothing.

---

[1] Satires

And we have learned by experience that libells & pasquills (the onely weapons of some unhappy p[er]sons) have been perennial to the ruine & distruction of the bravest men.

Be sure to have an Ephimerides[1] to know how the great Orbs of the Court move: & if any new star shall arise out of the East, & men begin to worship it, you must comply with the first, or study how to eclips & surpasse it, therefore it wilbe prudence to cut of[f] all steps by which others may ascend to height or grandeur, for if you leave any Sta[i]rs standing, others will climb up.

In all your negotiations you must have an undiscernable way of intelligence, as angels have of communication, Gygis' Ring[2] will be of great use to you for he observeth best who is least observed himselfe.

And if you designe your own safety, ever speak truth, for you will never be believed & by this means your truth will secure you if questioned & put those you deal with, who will still hunt counter, to a great loss in all undertakings.

Admit none into your caballe but such as have their fortunes wholly & solely depending upon you.

In dangerous attempts put others before you to act, but ever keep yourselfe behind the curtain.

---

[1] Ephemeris - gives the position of astronomical objects at a specific day and time

[2] The Ring of Gyges. Greek Mythological artefact mentioned by Plato. It allowed the owner to become invisible

In doubtfull matters, be ever provided with some cunning strategems, either to baffle your enemyes, or els to secure yourselfe and your own p[ar]ty.

If by wisdom you cannot attain your ends, use argument as they never fail; and, as men have a touchstone to try Gold, so Gold is the touchstone to try men.

I have hinted those things to you not that you should act any thing against honour or the dignity of your Religion.

Prudence is an armory wherein are as well defensive as offensive weapons, of the first you may make use upon all occasions; but of the other onely upon necessity.

We know that the Apocrypha[1] is allowed to be digested into one Volume, with the sacred word & re[a]d together with it, but where it thwarts that which is Canonicall, it is to be layd aside.

Policy & Religion, as they [do]well together, so they doe ill assunder: the one being too cunning to be good, the other too simple to be safe; therefore some few scruples of the wisdome of the serpent mixt with the innocence of the dove wilbe an excellent ingredient in all your actions.

---

[1] Apocrypha - Biblical writings not considered to be genuine

But I have stained too much paper, I must, with Apollos 'manum de tabula'.[1]

If you be mounted on the pyramid of honour you must remember it hath but one point and the least fals step will hazard your fall.

If you chance to loos yourselfe in the empire of greatnesse, returne to your own solitudes & privacy, & there you may find yourselfe again.

Let no condition surprise you & then you cannot be afflicted in any; a noble spirit must not vary with its fortunes, there is no condition so low but may have hopes, nor any so high as to be above the reach of fears.

In your worst estate, hope; in your best, fear; but in all be circumspect; man is a watch which must be lookt to & wound up every day.

It no lesse becometh the worthy p[er]sons to oppose misfortunes than it doth the weakest children to bewail them.

It is the duty of a brave soul always to hope, adversityes are born with greater glory than deserted, for such are the comforts of unhappy vertues & innocent souls.

It was a rare homage to Eumenes[2] whose courage no adversity ever lesned, nor p'perity his circumspection; one month in the school of affliction will teach you more wisdome than all ye

[1] Hand of the picture - do not further touch-up the picture
[2] Eumenes - Greek Scholar who accompanied Alexander the Great into Asia

grave precepts of Aristotle[1] in seaven years; for you can never judge rightly of human affaires, unless you have first felt the blows and deceipts of fortune.

I am not, I blesse my stars, dysturbed at any thing, nor doth passion disquiet me, I hate nothing except it be hated itselfe, & I am no more troubled for the want of any thing I have not, than becaus I am not the Sophy[2] of Persia or ye Souldan of Babilon.[3] He is a happy man that can have what he wills, & that I professe myselfe to be, because I desire nothing but what I can have.

However, 'innocence sit animus in irata fortuna'[4] for vertuous persons like the sun appear greatest at their setting and the patient endureing of a necessary evill, is next to a voluntary martyrdome. Adversity overcom is the highest glory &, patiently undergon, the greatest vertue.

And should you fall from your Prince's favour, yet you may be Rex stoicus, a king in our own microcosm, & he who knoweth how to rule that welle may dispise a Crown: thrones are but uneasy seats & Crowns splendid cares.

The chang of your fortune may diminish your hopes, but it will increase your quiet, you must understand that favourites are but as counters in the

---

[1] Greek Philosopher and Scientist
[2] Sophy is the English term for a Persian Monarch
[3] The Sultan of Babylon (or Sowdone of Babylone)
[4] Innocence is to turn into angry fortune

hands of great Princes, raised & depressed in valuation at pleasure.

There is no constancy either in your favour or fortune, or in the affection of Princes, so that no wise man can trust the one or depend safely on the other.

But whatsoever the traversers of fortunes are, let not discontent suppresse you; if the thing be within your power, manage it to your content, if not, it is an argument of weaknesse in you to be disquieted.

Do your best that your best may happen out, if that doe not yet think is best, however it wilbe piety in you to submitt to divine providence.

A humble soul like a white sheet must be prymed to receive what the hand of heaven shall imprint upon it.

Never anticipate your own misfortune for many times men make themselves more miserable than indeed they are, & your apprehension of infelicity doth more afflict that infelicity itselfe.

Hope wilbe your best antidote against misfortune and God's Omnipotency an excellent reward to fix your soul.

If you be not so happy as you desire, it is sufficient you are not so miserable as you deserve; if things goe not so well as you would they should have done, it is well they are not so ill as they might have been.

If you seriously consider you have received more good than you have done & done more evill than you have suffered.

Measure not life by your injoyment of this world, but by the preparation it makes for a better:

Looking forward to what you shall be, rather than backward what you have been: believe me he that anchoreth one thought on any thing this side heaven wilbe sure to be a loser in the end.

To serve God & keep his comandments is the onely wisdome & will at last, when your account of the world shalbe cast up, be found to be the best preferm't: & high happiness.

And so fare well, remember your mortality & eternall life.

(This final sentence in bold was added later and is in Martin Bladen's hand-writing).

Finis.

APPENDICES

As an Addendum to his own words of 'Advice to a Son', Nathaniel included in his essay to his son Martin a translation about the difficulties of serving a noble family.

It is clear that he was trying to influence his son away from choosing this as a career path and the lengthy translation was intended as a warning. Nathaniel had, of course, first-hand experience of working for noble families and so the following was included to reinforce those comments he had already made in the 'Advice'.

Translated out of Lucien's De Mercede Conductis: Of the inconveniences they suffer that serve in noble familyes; but more especially of those which gentlemen meet with

I know not where to begin to recount to you my dear Timocles, what they endure that serve in great familyes, tho' at first they are introduced as friends, whether it ought not to be called rather slavery. For I am a little acquainted with their suffring, not by my own experience but by what I have learnt from such as have been under such engagem't. From some who yet languish under those chains & from others who being enfranchised do with delight recount the history of their misfortunes & especially of their deliverances. These seemed to merit the best credit as being instructed by experience, having fully founded (if it may be sayd) these messages. I harkened to them with the same attention one does to such as relate their deliverance from shipwreck, the horror of the rolling waves, the raging of the wind, the terror of the rocks, they were ready to split upon, the dreadful cryes of the mariners when they saw the ruddor swept away, the mast broke & the sails torne in pieces, & all hope of safety lost; which is the very point of despair, the favourable conciliation of Castor and Pollax approved & restored them to the Cape of Good Hope, no Poet every layd the scene of a comedy more surprising.

Thus have I been entertained with the Tempests of the court, where every thing seemes to smile upon you at the first, but the calm is quickly turned into a storm and great loss with peril during the whole time of your navigation, & your vessel runs infinite risq of being dashed in pieces against some such thing liyes hid under the water, or ag[ain]st some sharpe rock, where after much danger, having lost all you may take it for a felicity to escape with your bare life. Yet in this doubtfull relation, methought they passed over in silence for very shame many thanks so I could easily devine, &

when amongst the rest I will represent to you, because I see you inflamed with a strong impatience to embark on the sea. For calling to mind one day that the company were falling upon this discourse, one there p'sons magnified the sort of life as the most happy, becaus they not only fared deliciously at others cost, lived in stately houses, rid in fine Coaches and kept company with the nobility, but were also payd for this, as for some great service: I observed people so enchanted with this discourse that they seemed ready to bite at the hook. Therefore that you may not be ensnared, & that you may not complain that I suffered you to tumble upon this precipice without due caution, I will rep'sent to you some part of the infelicityes inherent to this course of life and discourse to you the snakes that lie hid amongst these flowers.

After that enroll yourselfe in this forlorne if you please, I shall not be so much concerned since I have discharged the duty of a friend. However this discourse was intended particularly for you, it does not regard only Gentlemen but may be of use to all persons of good education that embarq in the service of noblemen, & receive their wages, learning the inconveniences they suffer are comon to all; but are more grevious to Gentlemen, which they find themselves treated without distinction. And here I do not so much blame those who are the cause of their sufferings as I do those that are so mean spirited to endure it: which ought not to take this ill except if they think it a crime to speak truth freely, since their infelicity arises from themselves, not me. Nevertheless I pretend not to comprehend courtyers within this rank, nor those other poer soules that know no better, and must either do that or nothing, being good for nothing els, for besides that they deserve no better usage, not regarding the truth when they hear it, they would not think you affront them tho' you throw a chamber pot upon their heads. It is therefore for the sake of Gentlemen I write, that they may enfranchise themselves if they please. Therefore I shall examine all the reasons that may induce them to this course of life, & shall make it appear that they are neither compulsive nor necessary to the end they may have no colour of excuse left.

Their first argument is poverty, the most intolerable of all evills which to avoid, everything ought to be attempted: then they quote Theogorus who says, it subdues the greatest courages, & aleged all that the Pocks & other mean spirits could invent to make men affraid of it - which it is very true if hereby they could find sanctuary, for their whole lives ag'st necessity, they would be excusable in seeking protection by this means from so potent an enemy: but generally the remedy is worse than the disease, & instead of caring it gangreens the sore; for poverty & the necessity of servitude endure still;

because in great men's familyes they expend their wages and often times lay out then owne substances too, which will stand upon account but never be paid.

Another reason why they embrace this sort of employm't is for want of some other profession & so before they are of age to understand it, submitt to this yoke of servitude. Let us examine then if there be not other more p'ferable ways of subsisting, & if this cost them not more than they get, & if their labour be not greater than a thrashers; for their chief felicity is to live in sloth splendidly. But it ever falls out crosse, for every day produces further infelicityes, insupportable both to flesh and blood (to the body and mind).

We will speak of this hereafter, & now briefly represent ye heads of them suffering: it shall suffice at present to show that these are not the true causes of them embarking, but that which indeed inveigles them in outside gallantry, the false show of wealth, these things blind their eyes and they imagine that true felicity consists in luxury and they promise themselves mountains of gold which they never enjoy but in their dreams.

It is not so much their necessity that proffers them as the desire of vain and superfluous things, that renders them slaves all their lives. For as the experienced courtisans knowing that enjoyment extinguishes the flower of love, entertain their gallants with protracted hopes, ever promising which they never intend to performe, so great men recompense those that have served, but if ever that by their expectation they shall be obliged to their services. Then at a ridiculous to suffer continually for bare hopes, especially since the reward is so uncertain and the evills of servitude certain: for I should not condemne them much for pursuing their pleasure, if they buy it not at the price of their liberty which is far more inestimable & instead of felicity embraced a shaddow. Thus Ulyssus his campagn men charmed with upfront pleasure, abandoned their honour & their native country, & they do little less than make their servitude under the name of reputable friendship. For my own part, I should despise the friend'p of the greatest Emperor, if it must cost me my liberty, for whilst he enjoy all the advantages of richness & greatness, I must remain poor.

Behold then the true reason of their slavery & the small advantage that arises from this course of life. Learn now for what methods they are compelled to take to gain this station, let us examine as they undergo whilst they are in it, lastly what is the fatal end of the Tragedy.

We must confess that it is no easy thing to gain admittance to the noble familyes, or that it is appointment as soon obtained as thought of; you must solicit diligently & make great many friends, clothe yourself according to the fashion & above your condition, least you should present before their eyes a disagreeable object, nor ashamed of you, you must attend him wherever he goes, through a thousand inconveniencyes, you must constantly attend at their rising, to have the honour to help them and endure the rudenesse of their servants & the refusalls of their porters, and give them money to retain your name. And after all this the great Don perhaps scarce designs to look upon you; but if after long attendance he shall chance to cast his eyes upon you & condescend to speak to you, then you think your fortune is made.

In the mean time those about him look upon you as some impertinent dull fellow, uninstructed how to behave yourselfe before persons of quality for which you call modestly a courtier calls speaking with want of tener and knowledge of the world. Then you retire out of countenance, and accuse yourself of faint-heartedness. In time, after great industry used, neither for heven nor a crowne, but to be enrolled a slave; if fortune smile upon you, and your stare favours you, then tryall is made of your abilityes. Then you choos his Lord[shi]p for the theme of your panegyriak, for these great men are willing to have their prayers published. How then do you strain yourselfe, as if your life and honour lay at stake, to make an accomplyshed piece in his prays, lest you should discover his

L[or]d[shi]p's expectations, then after his refusal, no person should receive you. How do you then torment yourselfe to excell your Rivall, & tremble if his Excellency does not approve of your composure, or play it couldly or not harken to it attentively. But you are transported with joy; when he smiles & makes you believe he knows it with satisfaction. Consider then what a displeasure is for a wel-bred man that understands himselfe to undergo the censure of some deliberate sot. And to this then they rip into all the actions of your life and arraigne the failures of your youth; for you shall not want such bad friends as will informe of all your follyes, either for malice or to get into your place, & the ill shall ever gain more credit than the good.

But if you are so happy to conquer all these difficultyes & that no person is able to undermine you, that you become acceptable both to the Lord'p & his Lady approves of you, that their friends & the whole family likes you, then you think you are above fortune, but alas you are full as ye bottom of the wheel, for ever then all your good is but imaginary, but your misery is real. Then it had been something if after all your pains you had undergone that ye had not only carried this Garland of Honour but some substantial profession also. For to begin with the beverage of your reception, permit me so to call the first report you take in the noble mans house: even there ye shall find greater cause of regret, than satisfaction. Immediately there comes a spruce servant to innur to you for which you ought to present him, which at first he may refuse but afterward will accept, laughing in his sleeve, to see you obliged to present him, for having become a partner of his servitude, you then prepared and put on your best clothes to appear at a feast where you ought to take your measures carefully, that ye neither come too early nor too late, for the one is unciville and the other importune.

The steward, after a civill reception, takes you by the hand, and presents you above him, to show you the more respect and after many complements you shall be compelled to take your place amongst several friends he has invited to entertayne you. Then, as if you were at the table of the Gods, ye shall feast your egoe more than your stomach, for observing well pathos, and they again are no lesse curious to remarck all your motions, & that, perhaps by order, to see if you regard any irregularityes in the Lady or the Children. And if you appear never so little surprised, or discomposed, they'l not fail to laugh yet to scorne, & take you for a Clowne, not used to converse with persons of quality. Nor yet scarce have the confidence to call for wine nor to carve for yourselfe but look upon some other to do as they may, lest you should comit some incivility. During this you are agitated with a thousand apprehensions sometimes admiring the Lords magnificent housekeeping, and despising your own condition in comparison with his; then again you blesse your good fortune that you have arrived to the enjoym't of these felicityes, & to live in such plenty all your life after. Then you think all your travells well imployed that you have arrived to this point.

Here they fall to drinking of healthes & someone taking a huge glass to doe you the greater honour begins your health, giving ye some title which he knows will be agreeable to you, but when it comes to your turne you are at a losse how to behave yourselfe, whose health to drink, & you pass for an ill bred fellow. You being thus treated at your first coming, raises a jealousy in the ancient servants. Aye say they, we wanted this piece of servitude, no body is valued, no one respected but this stranger, wherefore have we taken such care to accomplish ourselves. Mark then issue of it, sayes another, this will not last long, this is a new blosome which will quickly be cast behind the door, we shall see him in a very few dayes lame in his condition which as a great regrett as we do ours. Do not you observe, sayes another, how greedily he eates and drinks, as if he had never seen good victualls before. How he gnawes his bones, sure he never had his belly full of bread.

The truth of it is you make all the discourse, & as all the entertainment of the family, & his property & the feast where you are having eat and drunk above your ordinary custome, you find your stomach overcharged & would be glad to be out of the company, but had rather burst than comit so great an incivility as to break company; but to your displeasure the feast continues & still comes in fresh dishes (for the Lord is delighted to display to you his great magnificence) then ye curse a thousand times the feast and ye the Company, & the house you ever came there, & wish the house on fire, or some such accident, to disperse the company, that you might retire. You take but little pleasure in all that passes, dancing & musick, though in complaisance you applaud which you regard not, only that you may not pass for a sott. Judge now whether this disorderly feast, so much longed for, be halfe so desirable as a moderately furnished table with quiet at home: for it is not many dishes & variety of wines that makes the feast, but freedome & mirth.

Then reflect upon the ill consequences of those great entertainments, the head and stomach so disturbed, that ye cannot sleep nor forestall the night. The next day you must discourse above your salary, the maker of your servitude, & this before 2 or 3 of the gentlemen that supped with you, having then taken a chair for otherwise the Lord'p will not speak to you. My Lord begins thus: you serve the house where I live, hearof is the greatest freedome imaginable which you ought to take, & believe all I have is at your Service. It cannot be imagined that I should suffer him to be ill treated, or have any reserves from a person, to whom I open all the secrets of heart, & in whose conduct I have comitted my children, & myselfe; but since I am resolved you shall have some certain salary for your support, though I am well satisfyed that is not that which invites you to undertake this imploy, be so kind to speak freely what you expect, & dispose of the purse of a person that loves you, & your fee & lives at very great charges. I scorne to tell you what just expectation ye may have of persons will be made here, tho' they will amount to considerable, nor of the interest you'l gain by being with me.

This discourse unplanned and mighty hopeful precipitates you from the height of glory to which you thought yourself advanced, to the abisse of nothing. Tis some time before you are able to make any answer, you were so flattered with the hopes of an uncertain reward, & with his Ldshp's fair promises, which were nothing but the first complement of assuring you all he had was at your service, you tell him, in great confusion, you will trust his generosity, & accept of which his Lord'p pleases to allow you. But his Lord'p, not satisfied with the answer he presses you further and upon your refusal urges some of his friends upon which, after a long preamble of their greatness of his present new office, and expenses, to urge you to a more positive answer. Then this accomplished man, trained up all his life in flatteryes and courtship, entertayns you first to a congratulation of your happiness, that you have arrived at a post so desired by most persons, & you are received into the house & friendship of one of the greatest persons of the nation: he wills that you are happy if you know how to value it; that he knows several persons of eminent worth & learning, who would give a great deal to be in your place, for the honour & the advantages they could make of it, without demanding any reward for their paines.

After all this, he proposes to you some inconsiderable salary (especially if he can bait you with hopes) which you are obliged to accept, being ashamed to barter for more like a hireling, & besides that you are already too far engaged to retreat. You then become a slave, & enter upon your imployment which seems agreeable enough at the first, for they will not get cast into despair: they have some respect for a new comer, & are not yet weary of you.

Now you are congratulated by your friends and acquaintenances, as one that hath absolutely made a good fortune and those silly fooles that see your freedom in going into his Lordship's closet admire your felicity, though you yourself grow quickly weary of the honour & wonder what it is that they admire in your condition.

Yet you are hooked with these little applauses & judge of your owne felicity by the opinion others have of it. Thus you helpe to deceive yourselfe, hoping your condition will be daily bettered though find the contrary by experience, at last acknowledge all I have said, that all your advantages are imaginary, but your miseryes reall. Perhaps you will ask me what those infelicityes are, & what it is so insupportable in this condition.

First then you must bid farewell to all the glory and reputation derived to you from your ancestors, tho' now so great & reckon this day as the last of your liberty, the first of your slavery: be not offended at the word since you suffer the thing, & assure yourself that your services will not be so satisfactory as other mens; for having been accustomed to freedome you must needs performe them with a worse grace. Nay the remembrance of your former will often destract your mind & make you endure your slavery with the greater impatience for it is expedient you do not believe yourselfe a slave, because you have not been sould in the public market by sound of trumpett, but what need of that with your soule gets sould. Add to this how you must attend from time to time to get your usage & your financial power with the inferior servants. Now tell me how miserable wretch; for so I cann't forebear calling you, if you had been taken at sea and sould by pyrates would ye not have accursed your fortune. If we had been forced into slavery by any one would not you have appealed to the Governm't for succour & have called the Gods & men to witness that you were borne free. Yet after all this, for a trifle, you voluntarily renounced your liberty, & at an age when had you been a slave you ought to think how he obtained his freedom.

Where are now all those fine Philosophical discourses which extoll Liberty so highly, she herselfe is confined by your indiscretion & even vertue & wisdome by your conduct are rendred ridiculous. You eat every with the rabble, where you are forced to drink more than you have a mind to, & at their pleasure, & commend what you do not approve of. To be called out of bed the next morning by sound of a bell at daybreak, to loos the sweetest hour of your repose, to run up & down the towne with yesterdays dirt upon your shoes and stockings was always reduced to so great a necessity, that to live you must forgo the pleasure of life, & betray your liberty & your honour, or was ye dazled with the false lustre of wealth, or charmed with the s[c]ent of the kitchin?

You may repent at leasure the pains of your intemperance, & serve as a laughing stock to others, having the satisfaction to eat your bellyful. What do you think now of those admirable haranguers of wisdom and of virtue? I fear you have forgott them as much as your country and family. Thus to your slavery is added shame & to the troubles you undergo, disgrace & infamy.

But let us examine if the uneasiness of your condition be supportable, & if it is different from that of the meanest of servants. First then, the mighty passion your great Lord seemed to have for Learning was but feigned, for as the proverb says 'what has the Asse to do with the harp?' Can you think he will ever break his brains with the wisdome of Plato, or the eloquence of Domophilnes? the wise. When noble men are not covetous of ambition, they are sensual, effeminate and brutish. What then makes him desire to have a man of Learning in his retinue: only his vanity that he may be thought an ingenious man. Your periwig & your pantaloons made you much more acceptable to him than your Literature. He has a great desire to be thought a man of sence, or at least a favourite of learning, therefore you must attend him on all occasions wherever he goes. And often times in the streets he entertains you with some triviall affair or other because he woulde be thought to employ all by his time well. Nevertheless, you must follow him all about the towne, and while he visits some of his friends, ye wait at the doore all alone for his coming out and intertain yourselfe with some book you carry about you, not having so much as a soat perhaps. Here you are obliged to attend till night having passed all day & when ye come home shall scarce find opportunity for now they no longer treat you with the respect as at first, some fresh comer is now entertained into your place, according to the custome of these great men, for who dispise their owne and admire other men's servants. You are now placed at a side table at a distance, as if you had no relation to the family. Nor doth they send you any longer the best meals & wines, a lean over-roasted pigeon or firag end of the meat must serve your turne, while they feed on the choice foul & fattest venaison; nay sometimes they will take from you what hath been sent you, & (to comfort you) you shall be told in your ear you are of the family. If there be any rarity you must not expect it to last, except you be particularly befriended by your cooke who perhaps may give you some outside morcell.

So it is intollerable, nay enough make one that has a grain of sence go mad, to see your inserous placed at the table, & send away whole dishes of meat untoucht for want of appetite; which you dare not so much as taste, debauch in the delicious wines whilst you drink none, such as are Decayed. Nay, & even of this sad stuff, you do not yet go belly full, for often the servants, when you call for drink, will neglect you pretending not to hear you & remove from you. But for your great honour they serve you in a gould or silver cup, add to the rest of your grievances, the affliction you will have to see some pimp or fiddler valued above you, then you retire dissatisfyed & melancholy cursing your fortune & nature that did not give you some agreeable faculty to make you esteemed.

You know not how to relate a jest or to treat them when they are dysposed to be merry: for in a word, if you keep your gravity you are insupportable and if you turne jester you become ridiculous, as a fool in a Tragedy. You then wish yourself a poet or astrologer instead of a philosopher, because of the great respect you see those people have in the houses of the nobility, that compose them love sonnets, or promise them riches & honors by calculating their nativityes. Whereas you are obliged to cringe and faune, & are afraid lesse some rich hawk should condemne you for not having sufficiently praysed my Ladys page his dancing or playing on the lute; for such an omission as this would be an unpardonable crime: then must you, to show your ingenuity, fall into extravagant flatteryes; for some ingeneous piece of flattery is expected from which to give a specimen of your wit & breeding but which is worse than all this, if you be of service, the great Lord chanceth to be jealous of you, how unsafe are you then, so that if you be not wholy disagreeable you are forced to sit with your eyes shutt at the table, as the King of Persia's attendants, lest they be stabbed whilst they drink.

Great persons have many spies & they apprehend not only with papers, but also that which was never said or done.

When you awake in the morning, & reflect seriously on your conduct, you are ready to cry out, 'miserable wretch', a policy have I quitted to place myself into the gulph of misfortunes where are all those vain hopes whereof I dreamt? Instead of Liberty I find restraint and instead of reproof, toyle & tumult. When shall I once live to my self having hitherto been at the comand of others. I am dragged about like a hoodwinked bear; for a pastime to others, & a punishment to myself; but the bell rings and again must returne to ye accustomed course of drudgery.

In the meantime the course of life, so contrary to what you have been used to lead, bring you into a consumption, or a complication of diseases, yet for all that you must endeavour to look cheerful and to overcome your discontents for if you take but the least eas, it shall be sayd your counterfeit to excuse you from your business; so that in tine you becomes a mear skelliton.

Thus far have I represented to you the inconveniences of the towne, & if you go into the country you meet with fresh disorder of another sort. First then, not to speak of others, it happens, by reason of ill weather or your too long staying for your coach, you cometh to said Inn, that all the lodgings are taken up & you must be forced to lye with the cook, or some footman and take it for high favour too that he grants you a part of his bed. To this purpose I will tell you what happened to one of the Stoics, a Philosopher that dwelt with a Lady of the greatest condition in Rome. Who travailling into the country seated him next her spinner ...... This was sufficiently ridiculous to see the Armoretta youngster, and your grave Philosopher in company; one in a sober, modest dresse, the other dressed like a courtyer, both looking out at the same. Thus all the way laught & sung & could scarce hold from dancing in the coach. And to add to the felicity of the Philosopher, my Lady praysed him, as the most deserved person in the company to carry her little lap-bitch, which being big with whelp, she feared might meet some unlucky accident which might make her miscarry, which made our Amoretta break a jest on him, saying the stoick was now become cynick.

Our philosopher was content to bear the raillery, least fitting his wit to his, he should have become still more ridiculous. What augmented the pleasureness of the sight was to for an aged, grave philosopher, with his long beard, carrying a little bitch, peeping with her head from under his cloak, licking his rever'd Beard; tis said she blessed him severall times, nay & that she layd her whelps in his lap. After this manner are men of Literature affronted amongst noble men. I have seen a grave philosopher compelled to do claime at a full table to make the company sport, every one breaking his important jest upon his harangue, & afterwards for a consolation gave him a fidlers almes.

If your Lord'p happens to understand enough to write either in prose or verse, this is a fresh torment to you for he will be sure to read them to you even at meat, yet must admire them though they be full of absurdities & applaud his faults for Rhetorical Figures, unless you will run the fortune of the county, & if the tyrant denyes who sent such as did not prays him to his contract, to the Gallows, calling them either malicious or traytors. There are others must be tould by you that they are beautifull and fair, as Adonis himselfe when indeed they are the most disagreeable & deformed in the world. But it is still worse than this, when the Ladies are vertuous & will be entertained by men of Learning, when they are dressing, or eating, & if she chances during this to receive a letter from her gallo.... you must then quit ye grave discourses of wisdom & vertue whilst her Ladyship writes here love letter. If you are presented by them with some pitifull present or money or guift, you must then in gratitude make a lofty Panegyrique of them wherein you must compare them to whatever is most glorious & charming: & you must be sure to reward your servant that brings you the first news, tho' the next morning they come in whole troops to feast with you, to all whom you must confesse your selfe obliged, tho' they contributed nothing & make them presents or they will depart. Ad to this that to get good wages which are lesse than nothing you must court the Steward & Comptrollers, not to mention those that have the governing stroke with Monsieur and Madame, for if you should ask for your salary you will be thought intolerably impertinent.

Notwithstanding all this, you will receive nothing that you have not already run afore with your taylor, shoe maker or apothecary, so that you will not have one penny in your pockett. And to crown your misfortune, you are exposed to envy & detraction for as the Lord grows weary of you becoming ould and more burdensome, he would gladly be rid of you, not only because you are a charge to him, but because also you now begin to expect from him the recompense of your long service. He wants only now the least false report to ruine you, and turne you out of his house even at midnight, & then of all your faithfull services you have nothing remaining but the gout, or some other incurable malady.

During this time you have not only laid up nothing for a rainy day but ye have forgott all your learning so that nothing can be said in your behalf to gaine you any imployment or fortune. Ad to this that you are now grown so old that you reasonable old overridden horses whose very skins are given to nothing. Further, when he hath expelled, he shall invent some crime to accuse you of, unjustly & it shall easily be credited for the hatred that he bear to people in distresse. Ad to this that it is his mistrust to ruin you, lest you should reveal the secrets of his hous; as the great have always some intrigues not to be revealed.

There remains with you then nothing but your great stomach and dainty palate of all your travailes, which you is an infalable monster & will at length devour you when you are able to feed it no longer.

But to finish the portraiture of this sort of life of life, like Cobus, I would borrow the pencill of Apollo or some other of the famous persons of antiquity; but for lack of them I will do my best endeavours. Imagine fortune, wasted on a lofty throne, surrounded with rocks and precipicies & thousands of people on every side endeavouring to ascend; so are their eyes dazled with her splendour & glory. Hope gaudily clad presents herselfe for a guide to those pore mortalls having on one hand Deceipt, on the other Servitude, & behind her travell and paine, who after having readily treated & tormented them and abandoned them to old age.

Then does calumny seize them & expose their naked, ashamed, disgraced, attended by a sad repentance, that delivers them up to despair. This is the true scene of the ambitious. Consider now if you think it eligible to follow their steps, who entring the gates of glory go out at ye postern of shame; what you do, remember the opinion of your wise man.

We ourselves are the sole caus of all those misfortunes whereof we falsely accuse the fates. This is an apologie for himself for having taken upon him the Charge of the Emperor and Lieutenant in Egypt, he seems to have contradicted his principles by his practice.

I have a long time considered illustrious Sabinus, which opinion you would have of me, to see me engage myselfe in the services of the Emperor, after having so decryde those that enter into the service of great personages. I fancy you cannot forbear smiling & saying with yourselfe, How! After hearing so much blessed servitude, to cast himselfe voluntarily into it, hath he lost his judgm't or his memory, thus to condowne his discourses by his actions! It seems he has been strangly blinded with the lustre of gold, to put on the chains because they were gilded; that he has had mountanous promises made him to caus him to chang counsells at his age, & has renounced his liberty which was so naturall.

Then to this methinks I see you add your friendly advice; you may remember (say you) that your discourse has now been publiq, along time, & well received of all that have seen it, & particularly of the warned, for besides that it is pleasantly writ, is exposes closely & delightfully, the greatest part of those defects which are found in that course of life & contains most wholesome precepts to prevent the men of Learning from falling into that snare, capable of entrapping the most circumspect.

But since you are caught yourself, think immediately of suppressing your owne work, & intreat the Gods, if they can, to give a draught of the Lether Lake to all those that have seen or heard of it, least they reproach you as they do Bellerophon,[1] to have been your owne condemnation. For know well you the truth I see no roome left to defend you, & you can make no answer to those that say you talk like an Emperor, but act like a slave that ye are magnificent in words, but mean in deeds.

Others will say it is not your power they have red, or that ye have, like [A]Essop's Faybles,[2] adorned yourselfe with the feathers of other birds, that ye act like Talathe the Lawgiver of Croton who, after he had made most bloody laws against adultery, being taken in bed by his sister, cast himself boldly into the fire, tho' they would have changed his punishment into exile, & that he had love for his excesse, a passion that triumphs over the wisest of men.

---

[1] Bellerophon - a hero of Greek mythology, a slayer of monsters
[2] Aesop's Fables, a slave and story-teller who lived in Ancient Greece 620-560

Thus after having declared against the service of great personages, you yourselfe engage therein, even in your old age, & are yourself excusable in that your servitude is voluntary & gaudy. That old saying of the Tragedian will be retorted upon you, I hate that wise man that is not wise for himself & compare you to those actors who make themselves admired by other representations of the personages of rogues and heroes, & are after all but paltry rogues, or like Cleopatra, that after having danced to the flute in mans habitt with great applaus, forfeited all this to run after a few nutts that were cast before him. So you after having playd the Caesar, & given laws to the greatest men have shown that you were nothing better than what you pretended, & that your Philosophy was only lip wisdome.

Bear then justly the badge of your inconstancy, & engage wilfully in that slavery, after you have insulted so haughtily over the unfortunate, whose poverty constrained them to serve; like the man who sould an infallible medicine for the tooth ache and was tormented in it himself. Behold here it will be thrown in my dish, to which, after having made my vows to Mercury the God of Eloquence, that he would assist me with words and reasons to justify myselfe, it is high time that I make answer: or that he would as a great orator, supply my imperfect defence.

But where shall I begin, shall I cast your salt on fate or fortune, the arbitration of the world, is that drag or whither they please: or shall I quitt that defence as too weak & ordinary. I will deny that it was for perform'ce that I was put into the service of the Emperor, but to assist him in the conduct of his estate, & to be usefull to the publiq, or for the high opinion I have of his value; but I am afrayd if I say so, least I should be accused of adding flattery to inconstancy & so redouble my crimes in lieu of diminishing of it; so that there remains no more, but to lay my fault upon necessity that hath no law, & to say with Medea[1] I see very well that I do amis but I am constrained by poverty, whose spurs are so sharp that Theoginos[2] pardoned any man that was would drown him or precipitate him from a rock to avoyd it.

Behold here the apology which may be used in my favour; but do not think that I will use such weak arms for my defence. Famine can never be so sharp in Greece, that we need go cultivate large deserts of Arabia, nor I so bad an orator to have recourse to so weak arguments. Let us then take another course & joyfully consider the differences between the service of grandees and that of an

---

[1] Medea was a sorceress in Greek Mythology, grand-daughter of the sun god Helios, and a figure that features in the mythological story of Jason and the Argonauts

[2] Theogenes, Greek Mythological figure who was believed to have healing powers

Emperor. Surely these are as far different as Heaven & Earth; for alltho' it is still service & reward the things themselves have no resemblance, the one is a melancholy slavery the other an honourable comand which you cannot condemne without blaming all the magistrates and governors of provinces and generals of armyes themselves who, as well as myself, receive salaryes from the Prince for the services they render him.

It ought not then to confound things thus different, because they are expressed by the same terms, nor rank in the same forme all those that receive pay of ye publiq for their travells and services, otherwise you will involve the very person of the Emperour, as I shall show you immediately.

Besides I have only reflected in my concern upon scholars, for all tho' they are to noblemen what we are to the Prince, & learned in the house as we are in the Emperor's courts, yet for all that they bear no part in the Government. If I would then disclose my condition, as much as you would undertake and undervalue it, I could say that instead of being a servant then I am Viceroy in Egypt, & am arbiter of that Province, deciding differences between parties & looking to the observation of the laws, the interpretation whereof is in my trust. Besides I do not receive my allowances from any particular person, but from the Emperor; not wages, like those of whom I have been speaking, but considerable appointments. Ad[d] to this that in discharging my selfe well I may arise to greater dignityes, whereas those others remain slaves all their lives.

But I go yet further and say that there is no person that doth not labour in some sort for reward, & the Prince himself is not exempt, for not to speak of the tributes which they pay him, which are as it were the allowances of Royalty; the statues & the temples which they erect to him, the prayers and blessings they give him are the salary & the recompense of his court, & his watchings; so that one may say (if it were not too bold a word) that his employ & mine differ in the quantity not quality & bare the same resemblances as little doth to great. Indeed if I had layd down for a maxime (as some Philosopher that a wise man ought to do nothing) then they had had reason to accuse me of having contradicted my own Rules, & offended against my own maxime; but if they ought to employ themselves in some things, as no man will doubt, what can they do better than to do service to their Prince and Country. Ad further that I make not profession of that supreme wisdom which some do and place in contemplation only, but of human wisdom agreeable to our nature and to our business, which consists in being profitable to ourselves & others, without being an useless load of earth.

I have chosen then an imploy consistent with my capacity & to the study I have pursued all my life, & which (I can say) I have acquired some Reputation. And I believe now you will not condemn me, since you are acquainted how I lived in Gaul when you came to visit the Western Provinces, that I took place amongst the most celebrated Orators & received great fees.

I wrote to you then in the multitude of my imployment to justify myselfe with you, weary of the value I had of your merit, & of your approbation, for others let them condemne me, till they are weary that shall never affect me.
Finis.

Anno Domini
1694

CONTRIBUTIONS BY MARTIN BLADEN

The vast majority of pages in 'Advice to a Son' were written by Nathaniel Bladen, except for two sentences, which have been highlighted in bold, written by his son Martin who was the recipient of the 'Advice'.

In addition, Martin added in six pages of his own. In the original essay, these pages were slotted in on verso sides of his father's document and, as such, interrupted the order of the essay. So to keep the 'Advice' in the intended sequence, they have been extracted and are produced here. They were not inserted with any relevance of topic in mind and so their separation enhances the flow of Nathaniel's work.

The insertions by Martin deserve to be looked at separately because they were of a different nature, being words/phrases and parables that he thought memorable. Many come from the writings of Niccolò Machiavelli[1] and his publication 'The Prince'. For example:-

Martin: 'Whoever is the occasion of another mans

---

[1] Niccolò Machiavelli 1469-1527. Political writer. Exponent of the principle that Princes can justify (immoral) means if it serves their ends and that it is best to be feared than loved (for rulers). He also justified cruelty for a Prince leading an army as being necessary for his respect

advancem't, is the caus of his own diminution'.

Taken from Machiavelli on the subject of empire "Whoever is the cause of another's advancement, is the cause of his own diminution".

Similarly, Martin said: 'Tis weaknesse to believe that amongst great persons new obligations can obliterate old injurys & disgusts'.

Taken from Machiavelli on the subject of Great Persons "Tis weakness to believe, that amongst Great Persons new Obligations can obliterate old Injuries and Disgusts".

Martin: 'It is better for a Prince to be parsimonious than liberall'.

Machiavelli: "with time [the parsimonious prince] will always be held more and more liberal when it is seen that with his parsimony his income is enough for him".[1]

Martin: 'Reputation & Poverty make men industrious but it is the Laws that make them good.'

Machiavelli in 'Discourses on Livy' "hunger and poverty make men industrious, and the laws make them good".

Martin: 'Man is naturally wicked, never does well but upon constraints".

---

[1] Hume and Machiavelli: Political Realism and Liberal Thought by Frederick G. Whelan

Machiavelli: "most men 'are more prone to evil than to good" and *"The best means of habituating naturally wicked men to law and order is religion."*

It is interesting that Martin Bladen, who was just 14 when he received his father's 'Advice' should have demonstrated such a fascination with Machiavelli and his complex arguments on political theory, which some have interpreted as encouragement for republicanism. Martin would later, as Lord Commissioner for the Board of Trade be tasked with liaising between the King and his Privy Council and the far flung colonies where the power of Princes to rule was becoming increasingly challenged, such as in New England.

The next item Martin included was a reference to popularity from which Martin referenced the Gospel of Matthew:.

Martin: 'He that builds upon the People, builds upon the sand. Witness the Gracchi of Rome,[1] Georgi Seals of Florence; Earle of Essex in the reigne of Queen Eliz: of England.'
From the Parable of the House on the Rock: the Gospel of Matthew, part of the Sermon on the Mount .... 'Everyone who hears these words of mine, and doesn't do them will be like a foolish man, who built his house on the sand. The rain

---

[1] Graachi brothers tried to distribute land reform to the poor

came down, the floods came, and the winds blew, and beat on that house; and it fell - and great was the fall'.

Other inclusions by Martin perhaps were reflective of his studies at that time:-

"Let such as are forward to carry ill news to great men; remember that Sertorius,[1] the Roman Generall, slew a man of his owne that brought him ye news of the death of one of his great Officers, least the news should discourage the rest of his army.

Pythagoras[2] his lesson to his schollars was: do well and speak truth.

Demosthenes[3] says the greatest good that can happen to us in our life is to be Happy; but there is another thing not inferier to that & without which the first cannot subsist: to carry our selves with prudence; for grant that nature hath every thing requisite for greatness; yet if act do not conduct her, she is apt to foundre."

Another curiosity included in the 'Advice' and which appears to be in Martin's hand-writing is the following poem:-

---

[1] Quintus Sertorius, c123-72 B.C., a Roman Statesman and General
[2] Pythagoras of Samos, Greek Philosopher
[3] Demosthenes, c384 B.C. Greek Stateman/Orator

<u>On Woman</u>

Ye heavenly powers why did ye bring to light
That thing called Woman Nature's oversight
That she bread Tyrant full of misery
That guilded weather cock of vanity
A wayward forward & a constant evill
A seeming Saint sole factor for ye Devill
Were she proud Poxt painted errant hore
Patcht perjured plagued all ye were her no more
I could forgive her & connive at that
But she is wors & may in time forestall
The Devils proxy & damming of us all.

The poem appears to have been written by Martin, but yet the page is marked: MDCLXXI (1671) that being some 9 years before Martin was born. It may, perhaps, have been a poem written by Nathaniel and copied/written up by Martin later, but the style of the writing seems more consistent with the expression of a young teenage boy, which Martin was. It is assumed, therefore, that the date recorded (which is difficult to read with clarity) is in some way erroneous. Martin's views on 'Women' mellowed in later years and he went on to marry twice.

Lastly, Nathaniel's manuscript includes a poem written by himself, probably in earlier years. Father and son shared a love of poetry though they're styles were very different and they are displayed here, side by side, for comparison. Nathaniel's poetry, see below, was more mature and, it has to be said, was done with a purpose, that being to curry favour with Danby's 'tyrannical' wife.

To the Countess of Danby upon the happy recovery of the Earle of Danby from his late sicknesse

My faith is fixed, & now I alow we are
Of Providence the most imediate care;
If Guardian Angells, any thing believe;
Nay which is more hope now a kind reprieve,
From our deserved fate & punishment:
Since your great Lord restored to us is lent
Of heaven's love your living monument:
And tho' like you we doe no joy pr'tend
Yet we offer pyous thanks to Heaven may send
Blend them with you till they devoutly rise
And make up one Religious Sacrifice,
That may look well above & prove that we
For this last signall more thankful be.

So the Old Votaryes, though they could not come
To the dread altar with an Hecatombe,[1]
Yet the mean games which their devotion brought
Into one Pyramid of fire being wrought,
Tho' curld with your Great Smoak they lost their name
Yet kindled & maintained a Holy flame.
When in his sicknesse we did apprehend
Our want of merit might bring on his end,
When Heaven in Justice might withdraw the good
Which we (ungratefull) never understood,
All we could fear was just since lives for one
Raised to his height, for his great worth alone
In whose fair choice, great Charles at once did ...
His judgm't is as mighty as his love.
And now he stands ingaged to support
A drained Excheq'r & a rowdy Court
To clear his innocence, to allay ye heat
Of envy & ye malice of ye Great.
Faction to chock, religion to advance
And ye poor Royalist to countenance;
A work (though just since ye Great Martyn Jones)
No minister before ere thought upon:
He sees your old factious moles how ye work on
Hoping to have up a Rebellion.
From our necessity, & thus convinced
First make him poor, & then dethrone ye Prince.

---

[1] Hecatomb - great public sacrifice (of, say 100 oxen) in Ancient Rome or Greece

All those great Acts that singly would afright
A soul lesser active are but his delight
Who workes to save us, had effected it,
Would our ingratitude to heaven permit,
But our black sins are such that when his ....
I fear some fatall revolution;
Yet as loss piety did once withstand
The fall of Sodom & preserved ye land
So that ye Almighty could not on it powre
(Whilst he lived there) their last but angry showre
So all our fears wel so if time adjourne
That his Great Soul shall to his God return;
But with that day, fatall to us shall come
Which shall include ours & ye kingdom's domes
When to express our mighty loss are said
No more but those two dreadful words - he died
Where then, ah where shall miserable we
Find words fit to preserve his memory;
We'l borrow from ye Royall Martyrs Dust
And say - here lies ye Great, ye Good, ye Just.

- - -